A Man Is Not
A Financial Plan!

Galley Proof
May 2007

By
Sherry Allen Harrison

A Man Is Not A Financial Plan by Sherry Allen Harrison

Copyright © 2007 Sherry Allen Harrison

ISBN: 978-1-4276-1769-9

Printed in the United States of America

Published by Praxis Publications, Inc.

Introduction

The day Myrna came up to me after an investment seminar and said, "I know I can do this, but my husband won't let me," was the day I started writing this book. Like so many other woman Myrna trusted her financial well being to a man who, through fear, intimidation or simply custom had her believing she could not take care of herself.

Why do so many women go there? What keeps the vast majority of women from, 1) Taking control of their own financial interests, and 2) Creating substantial wealth? Men are much less likely to feel the need to be "taken care of." Nor do they seem to hesitate to make big money if they can.

What holds us back?

Over the last fifty odd years I have been single, then married long term, and finally divorced. I have been a fulltime Mom of three kids, a working Mom with kids and now a working woman on her own. I have been dirt poor, comfortable, reasonably wealthy, then broke again and now quite well off. In all of those years and under every circumstance life threw at me, I have taken responsibility for my financial security. Not every decision has been right or good, but I made them. The result is I have control over my life.

The purpose of this book is to give you the internal power to be in control of your financial health no matter where you find yourself today. What happened yesterday is over. What's going to happen in all of your tomorrows is under your control. That doesn't mean bad things can't happen. Of course they can. What it does mean is that you are the driver not the back seat passenger.

Let's begin by seeing how we feel about money, where those feelings come from and how we can dispel the myths that seem to guide our lives. From that exploration and understanding comes empowerment to change. Then let's examine the "how to's" of taking charge of our own financial future.

Get ready. Your life is about to change for the better.

Chapter 1

A Woman's Financial Place

Read these stunning facts:

- Women make less income than men.
- Women head approximately 50% of households.
- The vast majority of children are cared for and raised by primarily women.
- Too many children live below the poverty level in homes with single mothers.
- Divorce ranges between 45 and 50% of all marriages.
- Divorced women often face a lower standard of living.
- Women have a longer life expectancy then do men.
- Wives, rather than husbands, tend to delay or interrupt careers to raise children.
- Most wealth is controlled by men.

These are just a few of the facts that every women needs to know. Given these facts, it is time for women to take full financial responsibility for themselves and their children.

Taking full responsibility is a multi step process. We are all in different places in our lives. Our circumstances are varied.

The level of our individual awareness varies. What does not vary is the need to change our perspective on money and our actions surrounding money.

8 Steps To Wealthy Thinking

Step#1: Understand what we think or believe about money and why.

Step #2: Recognize the results of accepting less than full responsibility for our financial well-being.

Step #3: Decide to make changes.

Step #4: Gather the knowledge we need.

Step #5: Make a new plan.

Step #6: Gain the skills needed to implement our plan.

Step #7: Act on our plan.

Step #8: Accept wealth as our right.

This book is about the process of moving from wherever you find yourself now to a place of financial well-being. It is not scientific or scholarly; it is simply applying good sense and sound judgment to matters that determine our financial place.

We live in a land of unlimited opportunity. People from all over the globe rush to our country everyday to grab a chance at the opportunities that surround us all. Being a financially empowered woman is a choice. It is time for you to make your choice and make the most of your financial opportunities.

Chapter 2

Our Invisible World of Mythological Rules

We are all rule followers of the first magnitude. We learned to follow rules as children in kindergarten. A thousand little rules were forced into our behavior as kids and few of us know how to recognize these thousands of rules we've been taught.

For example, we all have rules that say, "don't challenge the authority of our elders." This rule makes it hard for us to make deals with people who are older, or in some way superior to us. Another example is that we all learned that "no" means "NO!" So when someone says "no" to us on some matter, our natural, trained inclination is to obey.

Among these thousands of "rules" are many that teach us about our roles and responsibilities in life. Some even inform us what values are appropriate.

Most of us are aware of these "rules" as they exist and exert their influence quietly in our world. For example we all recognize the "obey your elders" rule and the "no" rule. By recognizing them, we can consciously decide to "override" our learned inclination and act in defiance of those "rules" if it is rational to do so. The payoffs from taking a path outside of the "rules," even when we feel discomfort, are often well worth the effort.

A big challenge in navigating through our invisible world is recognizing all of the less obvious and apparent "rules" or "scripts," that we naturally and quickly obey. Rules, for example, like "father knows best" or "a woman's place is in the home." There are "rules" that, if left unexamined, can and often do have many unnecessary negative impacts on our lives.

Here are four commonly held notions. These four "rules" are powerful examples of pervasive sayings about men, women and money.

1. Money Equals a Man's Success

2. Money is Not the Measure of a Successful Women

3. Men Make Money, Women Spend Money

4. Men Collect Stuff, Women Collect Experiences and Memories

For many women, automatically abiding by many of the "rules" or "scripts" that populate this invisible world can have a dramatically negative effect on our financial well-being. These messages we faithfully but naively follow can cause a woman to lose her sense of financial responsibility. They also can restrict a woman from gaining financial success and wealth. In contrast the messages that inhibit women from making and effectively managing money actually empower men to build and control wealth.

It is "rules" like these four that, left unexamined, unchallenged and unrevised, can cost women financial freedom, control and security. Before women can make a responsible, rational financial plan for our lives, we must first look into the invisible world of learned "rules" and subconscious messages. We need to expose them. We need to determine the rationality of them. We must revise or rescript them. Only then can we take ACTION!

True success in life is about challenging not just what the rules are, but which rules you choose to obey simply because you've been trained to. This is specifically true where financial matters and women are involved.

It is our mothers, fathers, religions, and society that teach us the rules or scripts you and I learn. Both the message and the source contribute to the power that these learned rules have over us. Let's learn more about how these forces can control us if we fail to control them.

Chapter 3

Where The Rules Begin

Women are financially handicapped by up bringing, cultural attitudes, social mores, religious training and male-female relationship maintenance. We get messages verbally, subliminally, and from observed cause-and-effect. Advertising, books, plays and all forms of entertainment inform us. From the moment we are born, certain messages about how we should relate to all things *financial* are modeled for us. For the vast majority of women in Western Civilization these messages act to direct us toward financial *dependence*. However, in a world where women find it necessary to provide for themselves and often their children too, financial dependence is a disaster in the making.

We must examine, understand and reverse this reality. Women MUST become financially responsible and INDEPENDENT.

The Invisible Messages Are Subtle

As newborn infants some of the first things we hear and begin to internalize are messages from our mothers and fathers.

Susan smiles down at the squirming bundle in her arms and coos, "Sweet little girl, Mommy is here."

It's only been an hour or so since tiny Lisa was born. She has a head of feathery pale hair and trusting blue eyes.

Her Daddy, Stu, leans over and adds his words of welcome, "Precious baby girl, Daddy will always take care of you and make sure you have everything a little girl could ever want."

Even as baby Lisa's eyes work to focus, her hearing is already sharp and soaks in the crooning of her parents. The messages she hears will be reinforced over and over as she grow up.

In the next room, another mother and father are greeting their baby boy. There Rita tells baby Jimmy, what a big boy he is and how she will love him forever. . Jimmy is a tiny soft dark-haired boy, whose pale blinking eyes look toward the reassuring voices. Rita invites big sister Cindy to come closer and touch the baby.

"When we bring him home you can help Mommy take care of Jimmy," Mommy tells Cindy

His Daddy, Mike, tells Jimmy he will take care of him while he grows up to be a strong man like his daddy. These messages will be reinforced throughout Cindy and Jimmy's lives.

Let's look at and listen to these interactions very carefully. The messages are both of love and reassurance of course, but the *implications* are very different. Little Lisa is introduced into an environment of dependence where Daddy is the "giver" of material resources and where Mommy is the caregiver. It is Mommy who she will most likely model.

Baby Jimmy is greeted with words from Mommy that are strong and expectant, and by Daddy who will be his model to grow into a big, strong man.

For the purpose of this book we will be focusing on the impact of the messages communicated to females. However, the impact of the male messages cannot be ignored, because men and women must coexist. Each gender is not only affected by what they hear, but very directly by what the other expects.

Chapter 4

What Mommy Teaches Us

Through behavior modeling and words our Mothers communicate messages that instill in us the following attributes for relating to the male world:

- Care giving
- Deference
- Obedience
- Duty to family
- Communication
- Social Skills
- Conflict Resolution

While these are neither "good" nor "bad" attributes, the way women embody them as they develop their concepts of financial responsibility is our concern here. Also, because of the male dominated society in which we live, these attributes often involve the male-female dynamic.

In middle class America every home and every family is different in the details, but there are many similarities in how we interact with our children. Attitudes, social mores, cultural biases, and interpersonal skills passed on from one generation to the next, surface as we raise our children.

"Stu, Lisa's crying. Please check her diaper"

" Susan, come on. I'm working on the bills. I can't stop right in the middle of this. She really wants you anyway."

"Good grief," Susan mumbles, "Why do I always end up being the one to drop everything to change the diapers?"

"Hi pretty girl," Susan murmurs. "What's the matter? Your diaper's dry, so why are you crying so hard? Come on go with Mommy while I check on the laundry," she says while lifting Lisa to her shoulder.

"Stu, are you finished with the bills? Lisa's dry and quiet, so why don't you play with her awhile so I can start dinner."

"Ok, Susan, I'll watch her for you until the ballgame comes on."

Notice the dynamics in just this one small interaction:

- Daddy is busy with "important" work, i.e. paying the bills.
- Mommy is doing laundry and making dinner, which is not "important" work.
- Mommy, not Daddy, does the "dirty" work, i.e. diaper changing.
- Daddy is ASKED to watch the baby and Daddy agrees to "watch her FOR YOU…"

As these types of interactions are repeated in numerous variations over a number of years, Lisa absorbs these messages loud and clear, even if on a subconscious level.

"Oh my gosh, Lisa has a fever again, Stu. I missed 3 days of work already this month. Can you take today off to keep her home?"

"Susan, you know I have to be at the office for a big meeting this morning. Call your Mom. Maybe she can watch her."

"Stu, I can't expect Mom to be our babysitter just because Lisa's sick again. You need to help out here."

"But, Susan you know I can't risk MY job. Besides, your boss is a woman. She'll understand that you have to stay home with the baby."

"My boss might understand, but that won't keep her from firing me if I can't be on the job. We need both of our paychecks to make it, not just yours"

"Well it will be whole lot easier to replace your clerical job, than my supervisory one."

"You win, Stu. I'll call my boss. (While I'm home, I'll look for another more flexible job, since mine won't last at this rate,)"Susan thinks.

Lisa hears and sees messages that are going to influence her own life and financial prospects. Messages like:

- Daddy's job is more important than Mom's
- It is Mommy's RESPONSIBILITY to be the primary caregiver. Additionally, Grandma is a "natural" substitute for Mom.
- As is still most often the case Dad makes more money/has a more responsible job than Mom.
- Women universally understand that childcare is woman's work. Men expect other men to NOT be primary childcare givers.

As Lisa grows, she will not only see these messages repeated by Mom and Dad, but will also see the same things happen at her friends homes, on television and in story books she reads. By the time she is grown, the imprints will be deep.

"Mom," Lisa wails, "I hate homework! All of my teachers think they are the only one giving homework. My English teacher expects me to turn in my short story and Mr. Green, gives us 50 algebra problems to do the same night. I've been working on my story for a week like you told me to, and I almost have it like I want it, but how can I finish it right when I have all of this algebra to do. Ugh."

"Lisa, you can turn your story in the way it is. I'm sure it's good enough," Susan says." If you need help with your algebra, Dad will be home soon. Maybe he can help you."

"Susan," Stu cries walking in the front door. "I just got here. I'm too tired to do algebra."

"Lisa, you can do it and I'll give it a quick check in the morning before school. Besides, your grades are good enough to get into the state college, why are you worrying so much?"

Our school years bring the opportunity for even more messages:

- Women should are better at language arts than math and science. (Mom encourages work on story, Dad can help with algebra). "Good enough" is good enough
- Not as much is expected of women (state college)
- A woman's can "get away with" less than the best.

As she develops intellectually and socially, patterns are imprinted:

"Susan, who is Lisa talking to on the telephone? I hope it's not some boy."

"Stu, Lisa's 14 years old. What do you expect?"

"Well, I'm not letting my little girl hang out with boys. It's my job to keep her safe, so you tell her no boyfriends around here," says Stu as he stomps out of the room.

'Dad, Mom said you said I can't talk to Jimmy on the phone. That's stupid. I'm not a baby, you know, "Lisa declares.

"Well, baby, your Mom and I just want you safe and sound. When you're a few years older we'll talk about this. Someday you'll find a nice young man who will take care of you, but for now, I need to protect you," Stu proclaims.

Here we hear the strong message that:

- Girls are somehow weak.
- Girls need a grown man to "take care of them."
- Women are intermediaries. Dad dictates, Mom is the messenger.

Throughout her life Lisa is apt to internalize the messages that her parents model. As a female, Lisa will likely recognize her Mother's model as the one she is to copy.

"Lisa, I set up a bank account for you to draw on while you're at college," says Stu. "Every month I'll deposit enough for you to be able to buy books, food and such. If you run short give me a call and let me know what you need. Also, don't forget to take your car in for an oil change in about 5000 miles, since I won't be there to do it for you."

"Oh Sweetie," Susan begins, *"don't forget to write thank you notes to Grandma and Aunt Jeannie thanking them for your graduation presents. There's a Target nearby. That's a good place to buy the little things you'll need to dress up your dorm room."*

"Mom, which sororities should I consider pledging?" Lisa asks.

"I think all of them are nice groups of girls, so just pledge the one you feel most comfortable with," Susan replies.

"Hey," says Stu. *"I know a guy at the company whose daughter is in the best sorority there. I'll give him a call and get her name for you. It's good for you to have nice social group at school, but please stay away from the Frat houses. I don't want you getting dragged into any trouble."*

Even in the days heading up to college, the messages continue:

- Men take care of the money and automobiles, while women are in charge of social concerns and decorating.

- Men give specific referrals to the "best" sorority, while a woman gives advice to feel good about your choice.
- Men continue to warn against danger and "getting dragged into trouble, "because by implication a woman needs the warnings.

"Oh baby, you are such a beautiful bride," says Stu in awe of Lisa. "I'm so glad you found a nice man with good career prospects to take care of you. Now I can let go of my little princess"

"Thanks, Daddy," Lisa croons. "Jim is so much like you. I know I'm a lucky girl."

"Mom, did the flowers get here okay?" Lisa asks. "Can you adjust my train? It has to look perfect when I go down the aisle."
"Yes, Honey, everything looks wonderful," Susan, replies. "It's wonderful to see you so happy. I hope Jim will always make you so happy."

The wedding day messages continue to be consistent:

- A woman needs a man to take care of her
- A woman needs a man to make her happy

- Good career prospects for a man are paramount

Mommy is the natural model for the girls in the family. As these brief, but all too familiar bits of dialogue show, there are pervasive, consistent messages that we learn from our Moms. Many of these messages are communicated by the relationship between Mom and Dad.

If Mom acquiesces the majority of the time to Dad's opinions and demands, then we learn that this is how men and women are supposed to relate. In this way girls come to see that men are stronger, smarter, and more often in the "power" position in the relationship.

When Mom assumed the responsibility as primary caregiver, we learned that that is a "normal" female role. Mom's focus on social matters, while Dad focuses on family business issues, establishes our understanding of appropriate roles for men and women.

Although there are exceptions to and variations on the interactions between mothers and fathers, the pattern of what girls learn from their mothers is similar.

The main messages we learn from Mom are:

o Women are primary caregivers
o Women should defer to men
o Women are expected to be obedient

- o   A woman's first duty is to family
- o   Women are inherently weaker then men
- o   Women's role in the workplace is less important then men's
- o   Women are responsible for communication in a family
- o   Women are in charge of social, but not business matters

In later chapters we will observe how these messages play out in the adult woman's life and impact her willingness and ability to become financially responsible.

Chapter 4

What Daddy Teaches Us

The messages we get from Daddy and that are reinforced by our Mothers, teach us we need to use the following skills when dealing with the men in our lives:

- Compliance
- Compromise
- Concession
- Conciliation

From the moment we are born the main man in our life, Daddy begins teaching us how to interact with the male of the species. We learn that Daddy loves us when we are sweet, smiley, pretty and soft. As infants, Daddy will pick us up when we are freshly changed and powdered, quiet and agreeable. We instinctive know that fussy and messy brings Mommy instead.

> *"Mike," Cindy calls from the upstairs bathroom. "I really need some help. Cindy is out of the tub, running around naked. I can't leave the baby in the tub to catch her." Please come up and get her*
>
> *dressed for bed."*

"Alright, alright, I'm coming," hollers Mike. "Why do you always call me when I'm trying to finish up the report I need for tomorrow?"

"Mike, it will only take a few minutes, besides Cindy hasn't seen you for two days, because you've been working so late."

"Well, if I didn't work late when my boss asks, I might not get the promotion that just opened up."

"I know, Mike, but I work all day too and then have to get the kids ready for bed, not to mention cook, clean and do laundry every night."

"Rita, if you want to quit work, quit. If I get the promotion, we can make it ok."

Some of the messages from Daddy are:

- Daddy's job is more important than even his relationship with his family
- Daddy can and should be the primary provider for the family

- Daddy might AGREE to help with the kids, but they are Mommy's responsibility

We learn early that compliance and compromise keep things going smoothly. As we grow Daddy will rough-house with brothers, but not his little girl. He treats us as fragile creatures, so we learn to be conciliatory.

> *"Rita, call Cindy to the kitchen to help you. She keeps trying to get in the mix when Jimmy and I are wrestling on the floor. I don't want her to get hurt."*

> *"Mike, she won't break. She just wants some of your attention, too," replies Rita.*

> *"I'll read with her in a few minutes. Just call her in there for now," Mike retorts.*

> *"Okay. Cindy come help Mommy set the table for dinner."*

This common exchange communicates messages like:

- Girls are more fragile than boys, and need protection
- Girls belong in the kitchen (or another domestic arena)
- Daddy's interaction with a girl is intellectual not physical

Our role becomes clearer as we grow. If there is a brother in the house the contrasts are often quite vivid. Again conciliation and compromise by the females keep the peace.

> *"Mike, it's time to give Cindy an allowance, so she can learn to handle money. After all at twelve she is asking you for money all the time." Rita says.*

> *"Well if we give Cindy an allowance, we need to give one to Jimmy, too," adds Mike.*

> *"Jimmy's still pretty young, don't you think," asks Rita.*

> *"Not really. At Jimmy's age I was already cutting grass and making money. He really needs to learn how to handle it," exclaims Mike.*

This sends some subtle and not so subtle messages to Cindy:

- A girl goes to Daddy to ask for money, unlike a boy who could get a job
- A girl may need to know something about money, but a boy "really" needs to know
- Daddy is the source of money, not Mommy

- Mommy ASKS Daddy if it's time to give an allowance and Daddy makes the final decision

When the messages are specifically about money, the future impact on a woman's sense of her appropriate financial role becomes crystal clear. By conceding, even if by omission, that Jimmy's financial role is stronger than Cindy's, Mom again reinforces Dad's demand for concession.

When we go to school we are told, "be good." In our teens Daddy "protects" us from the evil boys.

> *"Hey kids," Mike prompts. "It time to get to the bus stop. Don't forget your lunches. Mom fixed them before she left for work this morning."*

> *"Okay, Daddy," says Cindy. "Wish me luck. I have cheerleading tryouts this afternoon"*

> *"You go girl," Dad replies. "Just imagine in a couple of years you could be cheering Jimmy on as he runs for the winning touchdown. How great would that be?"*

> *"She just wants to be a cheerleader because they get all the guys," taunts Jimmy. "The ball players love to have a cheerleader as their girlfriend."*

"Jimmy, don't pick on Cindy like that," Dad chides. "Besides, my little girl knows better than to get involved with those guys. If one comes here to see her you and I will just chase them away, huh?"

How blatant are these kinds of messages?

- Mommies fix lunches (not Dad who is still drinking his second cup of coffee)
- Girls look to Dad for reinforcement of their goals
- Girls play a secondary role to boys
- Girls haplessly attract boys and need protection by the Men in their lives

Here again the differentiation of proper roles is reinforced. The roles will have a definite impact on a woman's financial identity.

When it's time for college, Daddy gives us even more dubious messages.

"Rita, why is Cindy so determined to go to an Ivy League school?" demands Mike.

"Daddy, I've got top grades and look at my SATs. They are top notch," Cindy wails. "I know I can get in and maybe even get some scholarship money. If I'm going to get into Law School, I have to have the best undergrad degree I can."

"Cindy, your Mom and I want you to be happy, but we need to save money to send Jimmy to college, too," Dad, declares. "You will probably find a guy like your old man and get married and have kids. Jimmy needs to be able to provide for a family. So, we have to be sure he gets the best education."

"Cindy," says Mom. "I want you to be whatever you want to be, but we have to be practical, don't we?"

Picture the kind of effects this may have on Cindy's future financial mindset, not to mention financial earning ability. Messages like:

- Men need, and in fact deserve a better education
- Women are just going to get married anyway
- Women need a man to provide for them

When in our homes, we experience these types of daily interactions; girls hear, see and assume roles that are conciliatory, compromising, and compliant. Concessions to the males in our young world are played out in subtle and often not so subtle ways over and over again. When we take a look later in this book at some of the typical financial scenarios for woman, this early training will be evident.

Chapter 5

What Our Religions Teach Us

The major world religions are the foundations for our social and cultural mores, whether we are "religious" or not. The predominant religion-based messages impact a woman's view of herself and her place in society. It is often this view and sense of place that can dramatically impact women's attitudes toward financial issues. They can also influence a woman's opinion about money and its value. Some of the most often seen messages include:

- God will provide
- Turn the other cheek
- It is better to give than to receive
- The rich will have trouble getting into heaven
- Share all you have with the poor.
- The man, husband, father, even brothers, head the family
- Women are secondary to men

As religious messages these impart and provide, among other things, a moral basis for society. However, when women internalize these messages and implement them within the family, workplace and society, the messages can be distorted or misunderstood to imply submissiveness or even a disincentive to developing financial strength and independence.

As Lisa listens to her Sunday School teacher, Mrs. Swanton, read the memory verse for today, she is thinking about putting her nickel Daddy gave her in the offering basket.

"Lisa," Mrs. Swanton asks, " can you repeat the memory verse for us?"

"God loves a cheerful giver," recites Lisa proudly.

In the car going home from church, Mom asks, " Well, Sweetie, what did you learn in Sunday School today?"

"I learned that you have to give your money to the poor people," says Lisa.

"Good girl," Daddy adds. " Did you put your nickel in the offering basket?"

"Oh yes, Daddy. Mrs. Swanton said it would help feed the poor people."

The early messages are:

- Money is to give away
- It's Daddy's money we are using
- Some people in the world are classified as "poor" and are entitled to your money

None of this is "bad." But as Lisa grows the messages need to mature into honest, realistic and rational thinking. If that doesn't happen, a sense of obligation to give to others and, on the other hand, a concept of entitlement is formed. This can and will lead to lack of financial initiative and financial dependence.

"Mom why are you so sad?" asks Lisa.

"Don't worry, honey. It's just that I will not be working for Mr. Andrews' company anymore," says Susan.

"But why," demands Lisa. " Everybody knows you do all the work and Mr. Andrews just plays golf. What happened?"

"I really can't explain it, but someone got mad at Mr. Andrews for not paying him and he blamed it on me. Mr. Andrews never told me to pay the guy, so I don't know anything about it"

"But, Mom," Lisa cries, "tell everybody it's not your fault. That's not fair or right."

"I know, Honey, but what can I do? Like the Bible says you have to turn the other cheek and forgive. I'll get another job somehow."

"Oh Mom, I'm so sorry. But can I still take gymnastics lessons? I heard you and Daddy talking about how expensive they are?" wonders Lisa.

"Lisa, don't you worry about that. Daddy will figure it out. Besides, you know that no matter what, God will provide for us, right?"

"Sure Mom. See you after practice," Lisa says as she bounds out the door.

If Lisa is taking these messages at face value as her Mom indicates she hears,

- Daddy and God will take care of all the concerns including money for gymnastics
- Mommy does not take apparent responsibility to correct her own financial situation
- We will rely on Daddy foremost financially
- When wronged, turn the other cheek

Again there is nothing inherently "bad" or "wrong" with this scenario, but the implications for Lisa as she moves to adulthood are directing her toward a weak rather than strong vision of how she as a woman will fit into the world financially.

Across town, Cindy is sitting in church with her family, listening to the minister's sermon.

"Dad," she whispers, "why does Pastor Kenneth always preach the sermon and Pastor Linda say the prayers?" I heard Pastor Linda talk at Sunday School and she's more interesting than Pastor Kenneth any day."

"Cindy, be quiet. We'll talk about this later," Dad answers.

In the car going home, Cindy raises the issue again.

"So Dad, why does Pastor Kenneth do all of the preaching in church," Cindy demands.

"Cindy, of course Pastor Kenneth preaches. He is our senior Pastor," retorts Mom.

"But why is he senior, Pastor Linda's been at the church much longer than Pastor Kenneth and besides, I think she's smarter," is Cindy's indignant reply.

"Ladies," soothes Dad. "We need a strong leader like Pastor Kenneth to speak to the congregation. Everyone knows Linda is great. Heck, she manages all of the Sunday School, Daycare and Fellowship programs of the church. We couldn't do without her. But a man is who we expect to see in our pulpit. If Pastor Kenneth is sick or out of town, Linda always steps in and does a nice job. Also, we pay Pastor Kenneth a bigger salary than Linda, so we expect more from him."

"Besides," pipes up Jimmy, "everyone knows God is a guy, right. So the preacher should be a guy, too."

This brings a quick laugh to them all.

Messages of powerful importance are expressed in this exchange:

- Men are in charge of the important matters
- The perception that God is male
- Women are good at the administrative and less crucial jobs
- Despite actual seniority, the man "deserves" the "senior" title
- Men make more money
- Men deserve a title of respect from other men, while women do not

Whether you are associated with a church, temple, mosque or other group, you can recognize the truth in this dialogue. Even if you are not involved in organized religion, the media certainly reinforces this message. There are huge social implications demonstrated here, but we want to focus on just the impact this type of scripting for the female psyche will have on financial attitudes.

"Mom," whines Cindy, "I gave Jenny and Karen really nice birthday present, even though I only had a little bit of money, but they didn't even give me anything. Both of them are rich, too"

"Now Cindy, you know it is better to give than receive. Didn't you have a lesson about that in Youth Group last week?" asks Mom.

"Yes, but I gave all I had and they have everything, but couldn't even get me a little present."

"I know, Cindy, but you are the good person to give. The Bible says that the rich will have a harder time getting into Heaven," says Mom. "So, wouldn't you rather be good and get into Heaven?"

When the religious messages are put into this type of context, women are likely to adopt the position that:

- Giving is good
- Being wealthy is BAD
- Being selfless is right

If women are infused with these religious notions, coupled with Mommy's and Daddy's messages of proper roles, goodness, badness, rightness and wrongness, then the ways women play out their adult roles with regard to money and financial responsibility are negatively impacted. When Lisa and Cindy become wives, mothers, and/or businesswomen, the scripts that embody these powerful messages inform them. If the scripts contain visions of financial dependency and reliance on men where money is concerned, then the roles these women play will tend to go in that direction. As we explore the situations that adult women find themselves in today, we will examine how to rescript these messages to instill financial independence in our lives.

Chapter 6

What Society Teaches Us

"Get Motivated" was the headline on a full-page ad in this morning's newspaper announcing a "Dynamic Seminar to INCREASE YOUR PRODUCTIVITY and INCOME." It proclaimed "Motivation! Inspiration! Career Skills! Wealth-Building!" would be among the topics covered. This sounds all great until you see the faces of the nationally known speakers from the business, media and government arenas. ALL seven of the speakers are MEN. Not one woman is included in the lineup. The messages are crystal clear and disempowering for women.

Society and our culture are full of these types of messages that promote financial dependency for women. These messages are both spoken and implied. We hear and see displayed messages such as:

- It's a man's world
- Men belong in positions of power
- Men are better at business
- Men make money, women spend it
- Find a husband to take care of you
- The man makes more money

"Ronald, do you think the country is ready to elect a woman President?" asks the news show host.

"Well, Jim, I'm not sure if the country is ready to accept a woman President. If we thought the 'First Ladies' had too much influence on their husbands, imagine the concerns we'd have about the influence of a "First Gentleman." Ronald replied with a laugh.

"Yes, but how about a woman Commander in Chief? Can we expect a woman to be strong enough to commit our armed forces to fight? Or can a woman make the tough decisions a President has to make regarding terrorists?"

"Those are good questions, Jim. I also am concerned about how the other world leaders would view a woman, especially those cultures that are less accepting of woman, than we in the West are."

"Good point Ronald. In the dangerous world we live in, we need a leader who is strong, decisive,

and not afraid to make the hard decisions," asserts Jim.

On almost any Sunday morning we can see some variation of this exchange on television. Turn on talk radio and the same messages can be heard. Pick up a news magazine and this type of debate will show up. How can we help but be immersed in these beliefs:

- It is a man's world
- Men are stronger than woman
- Men belong in positions of power
- A wife should not be in a more powerful position than her husband

"So, the Morning News Show host asks his guest, a top grossing film director. "What are you going to do with all that profit? Have no fear," he responds. "My wife spends it as fast as I make it."

"I understand that," laughs the host. "My wife certainly knows how to spend what I bring home."

A light-hearted and widely acceptable exchange such as this certainly conveys a message of female financial dependency.

It also reinforces an image of women irresponsibly spending money. We are left with the stereotypes that:

- Men make money
- Women spend money that is not of their making
- Women, by implication, are not earners
- Women are irresponsible financially

Our Western society presents so many powerful images that feed negative stereotypes. These images and language mold a woman's view of her position in society and how she is expected to relate to financial matters. Other familiar examples include the following:

It's the opening bell on Wall Street. As Extraordinary Brands stock opens on the Big Board for the first time, the founders, Arnold Jenkins and Clinton Armand wave to the crowd on the floor. The trading floor is covered in a sea of mostly men, all wheeling and dealing. This is the symbol of financial power in the world.

In the latest edition of World Business magazine, is a listing of the Fortune 500 companies. The pictures of the CEOs of these companies include less than 20 women.

Today's newspaper leads with a story in the business section that features a picture of the owner of a local start up company, Henry Oliver, which is being bought out for $50 million dollars. Mr. Oliver's bio describes a man who developed an innovative product in his garage, while his wife worked to support the family. The implication is that Henry, but not his wife's contributions are worth $50 million dollars

A regional business journal states that the latest statistics still show men make more money in the workforce than woman. The article concludes that progress is being made, but since men hold most of the professional and executive level jobs in the country, naturally the numbers will show men earning more than women.

The nightly news features the powerful political figures commenting on the world situation. Since the vast majority of members of Congress, Legislatures and city or county boards are men, that is who we see on television news.

Walk into most banks or other businesses and we see women in clerical type positions, while men are in more of the management jobs. A man sits in the corner office, while the ladies take up positions at desks in front of those offices.

It is virtually impossible for women *not* to view themselves as weaker, less powerful, subservient, and less valuable than men. Even when we see women in powerful positions we are reminded that it is the exception rather than the rule in society.

The Atlanta Journal Constitution in it's "Issues" section Sunday November 26, 2006 poses the question, "Is it appropriate for journalists to write about Nancy Pelosi's clothes…" The mere fact that this topic is even worth discussing rather than the topics of governance and power that should surround the most powerful woman in American politics, highlights one of many subtle ways that women in powerful positions are "put in their place."

The messages that echo from these images are:

- It's a man's world
- Men are better at business and governance
- Men belong in positions of power

The impact of these powerful messages permeates every aspect of a woman's self-image, self-esteem, and self-actualization. Before we can rescript and reframe the mental messages that drive us or slow us down, we have to examine the validity of the messages.

With many of these ideas (men make more money than women, or the world actually is controlled primarily by men, etc.) we need to recognize that these truths are not true because of the way things truly are, but because this is how our society has historically developed. In other words we've learned it.

The changes we are seeing day by day in America indicate that more and more women are moving into positions of influence and power in all areas. Late in the year 2006 we have a woman Secretary of State and Speaker of the House. Plus, there are a growing number of women being elected to positions from the local to national levels.

In the business world women are CEOs and Chairmen of Boards of Directors. In our churches we see increasing numbers of female clergy. In courtroom the number of women on the bench and at the bar are growing daily.

As entrepreneurs, women are also coming on strong. Women are starting businesses of every type. Many are independent contractors. Industry groups such as Real Estate are becoming predominately female.

These changes need to re-form our internal scripts, telling us that women can do anything they wish. Rather than looking at how things HAVE BEEN for women in society, we need to instead look to *how they can be*. How they will be.

It's a great time to be a woman in America! Let's begin exploring how women in all positions of society are taking responsibility for their own and their family's financial well being. Women need to recognize the powerful impact they can have by learning to, and being willing to become wealthy.

The stories you are about to read are all true. I have changed names and details to preserve privacy in most cases. As you read about these true-life stories, imagine yourself in their place. Picture how you would have acted and reacted to the situations. Open you mind to the possibility that the rules and messages that directed them are also affecting decisions you are making in your own life.

Chapter 7

The College Woman

Rosie made top grades in High School and earned entrance into a top college. For the next four years she excelled in her studies (she was a Math major), became a leader in her sorority, and worked a part time job. Her social life was active and varied. During college Rosie met and fell in love with a great guy. Doug did well academically earning a Communications Degree and was a leader in his fraternity and worked in the summer for his family business.

Then came graduation. Also, there was an engagement ring. Both Rosie and Doug moved to Doug's hometown where jobs were more plentiful. After diligently searching for a good job, Rosie finally took a job working as a clerk in a retail store. Her boyfriend and now fiancé was offered a position in a start-up company with lots of future growth.

Rosie did all of the obvious things that are believed to contribute to future career success. Her boyfriend appeared to be preparing in the same way. So, why were their financial futures so different?

Myth: "Academic credentials are will lead to a good career, thus financial success"

It's better to have good credentials than not, but that is rarely what gets a person hired or promoted. Even a Math degree rather than a Communications degree will not necessarily be a strong determinant. There are clearly other more important factors. Have the credentials, but do not depend on them for financial success.

Myth: "The perceived value of sorority leadership positions is the same as a fraternity"

Sororities are what they purport to be, social associations. Fraternities, in contrast, are basic networking structures that have social activities. When women leave college, they tend to stay close to their sorority sisters until they have been bridesmaid for one another's weddings. Then women shift their affiliations to husbands and family.

Men, however, maintain their connection with fraternity brothers for a lifetime. These men consider their brothers to be valuable business associates who will continue to provide references, introductions, advice and powerful professional contacts. All of these things lead to a higher potential for financial success. Therefore, being the President of your sorority is viewed as qualifying you to organize social and charity events, plus it assures that your bridal party will be large. Unless women grasp the need for lifelong professional connections that are used to improve their financial prospects, women will likely make less money.

Myth: "It's what you know that counts."

Your IQ can be through the roof and you may win every trivial pursuit game, but unless the right people KNOW YOU, you have little. Notice, I said who knows YOU, not who you know. The higher your level of notoriety or celebrity, the better your chances are that financial opportunities will be presented to you.

Chapter 8

Young Single Career Woman

"Laura, can you meet me for drinks and dinner in town at 6 PM?" asks a hurried Dana. " I have some information about a new real estate project I want to talk to you about."

"I can do drinks, Dana, but I can't stay long enough for dinner. I have a meeting downtown at 7:00 PM," replies Laura.

"Ok, good enough, Laura. I'll see you at 6 then," says Dana.

At 37 Dana is a mover and shaker in the real estate industry. She sells high-end properties in one of America's largest cities. She is the "right-hand gal" of one of the most successful developers in the area. When she went to work for Simon right after college, he was just getting started as a real estate agent. Dana worked with him to create first a brokerage business and continued with him when he started a construction company. Now after 23 years Simon is a multimillionaire with communities bearing his name all across the region.

"Laura, hi. I'm, so glad you could make it," says Dana. "How have you been?

"Really good," responds Laura. "With the political races heating up, I am up to my eyeballs in campaign planning for the councilman. There's hardly anytime for myself"

"I know what you mean," laughs Dana. "Simon has got me running a mile a minute to get the plans for his newest development ready for the planning commission meeting next week. If I don't get everything in front of the commission by then, we may miss an opportunity to start construction this spring. That would not make him happy at all."

"So tell me about the project," encourages Laura.

"It will be huge and tremendously profitable," replies Dana. " In fact, I'm thinking about buying a couple of the town homes for an investment. Simon says it's time I built some equity for my

future. I guess he's right. Since I don't see a "knight in shining armor" in my immediate future, I suppose I need to do more than contribute to an IRA for retirement, huh? What do you think?"

"Well, Dana, Simon certainly knows how to make money, if he is encouraging you to do it, then I think you should," replies Laura. "I need to run now though, but keep me posted on what you decide. I might look into buying something, too."

For the last 23 years Dana played a critical role in Simon's business development. Not once during that time did she see herself in any role other than EMPLOYEE. Although even Simon admits to his friends that without Dana's talents and hard work he would never have gotten where he is today, neither Simon nor Dana ever view her as a BUSINESS PARTNER. In fact if confronted on this issue, Simon would explain that he has paid Dana very well over the years and has promoted her to highly responsible positions that have furthered her career nicely.

The reality, however, is that Dana still has a nice job, while Simon has a business empire and the wealth that comes with it. Why is this a typical reality? Some of the messages that inform Dana (and Simon, by the way) and lead to this situation are:

Myth: "Men are businesspeople, women are assistants"

We look around us and SEE that this is most often reality. The danger is in accepting this reality as the only one. Women have proven themselves to be very capable business people in every industry group. So, although the female business role models may not be as prevalent as the male ones, they do exist. Choose to envision yourself as businesswomen.

Had Dana seen herself in that role early in her business relationship with Simon, their "partnership" would have been much more likely to develop into one of true partners, both willing to take the risks and enjoy the rewards of building a successful business, rather than remaining employer and employee.

Myth: "If I wait, a man will come to take care of me."

More and more women are delaying or even foregoing by choice the traditional path of marriage and family. Since over 50% of all women either choose to be or find themselves by circumstance single, it's time to wake up to our own need to take responsibility financially for our lives. Living with the "invisible" notion of a "knight in shining armor" coming to our rescue is irrational and potentially disastrous. Take responsible for your own rescue from financial neediness and a shaky future.

Myth: "I'd rather be liked, than be rich

"The lessons we learn from infancy to be nice, sweet, and above all acceptable, are at play here. We must reexamine these premises.

"To whom must we be acceptable?" is the first question. Is it men in general? Is it to other women? How about being acceptable to ourselves?

"What is acceptable?" certainly needs to be answered. Does it mean being universally loved? It is having the respect of others? Does it mean seeing a positive reflection of ourselves in other's eyes?

"What are being nice and sweet worth?" needs addressing. Does it buy a smile and an occasional thank you? Can we use nice and sweet to pay the bills? Will these characteristics provide security and safety?

Change these messages to ones that are truly worthwhile.

"I can be rich without hurting others." Doesn't that make more sense?

"I am a good person, who works in the best interest of myself, those I love and the world at large." Isn't the concept of a good person, more meaningful than nice and sweet? Of course it is.

Remove the nebulous notion of acceptability from your psyche. Realize that it is to ourselves, and any Higher Power that we acknowledge, that we owe an accounting of our worth as human beings. Making ourselves successful, rich, happy and in harmony with our fellow humans is a much more rational message to follow.

Chapter 9

Young Wife and Mother

"John, please call the boys in for dinner," hollers Ruthie. "Make them wash their hands, too"

"Ok Sweetie" answers John.

Once everyone is sitting at the table, John asks, "Who has homework tonight? After dinner you guys head upstairs and get to it. Mom and I have both had busy days today. How about you guys? Anything new going on?"

Both of the boys give their normal, "nothin' new for me."

"John," begins Ruthie, "open enrollment is coming up at work for life and disability insurance. Will you take a look at the material and tell me what I need to do? It's so confusing to read and you've been through this already at your work."

"Sure, Ruthie, I'll take a look before bedtime," replies John willingly. "Did you get by the cleaners and bank this afternoon? I need to pack tonight for the trip to Dallas."

"Yep, " says Ruthie. " I got cash for your trip and all of your shirts came back on time for a change. By the way, when is your office party? I need to find a babysitter and pick up a hostess gift for your boss's wife."

"Oh yeah, good thinking, Ruthie. It's on the 15th and I heard one of the guys in the office say old Jimbo likes his Jim Beam. That might be a good gift," added John helpfully. "Is your company having a party this year?'

"It's happens to be on the 15th, too," replies Ruthie.

"Oh well," says John, "I guess we'll just have to miss another one."

"John, you know I'm in line for that promotion to group manager. It won't look good if I skip out on *the party. All of the other managers and Human Resources people will be there. It could give me a great opportunity to rub elbows with the big wigs,"*

"Yeah, but you know I am expected to show up at the big gala with my beautiful wife on my arm. I have to keep up my image, you know," teases John. "Anyway, if you tell them you can't make it because babysitters are hard to find this time of year, they'll accept that. It shouldn't hurt your chances much."

"I guess you're right," replies Ruthie. "Let me get dinner cleaned up while you look at those insurance papers for me."

In just this brief glimpse into Ruthie and John's life, some dangerous little mind messages entrenched in Ruthie's being show up.

Myth: "A husband's job and image are most important"

In a two-income marriage partnership, is it rational to always accept this as truth? Certainly not. When both partners have a job, it is because they need the income of both, OR both have chosen to maintain careers. In either case, both jobs are valuable both to the family's financial circumstances and /or to the personal needs of the individual.

Decisions that impact both careers must be given full consideration. Do not accept deferring to a man's job or ego out of habit or instinct as right.

Make carefully weighed judgments based on the optimal outcome for everyone. It is only then that you will be taking full responsibility for yourself. A decision to miss an office party that costs Ruthie a promotion can have a lifelong financial impact.

Myth: "Men understand complicated business issues better than women"

Anyone who takes the time to read and learn about any business matters can understand them. Accept that you are responsible for knowing about things that affect your financial well-being and get the knowledge necessary for understanding and good decision-making, then this myth disappears.

Chapter 10

Promises and Dreams

Tara thought she'd made it through the really tough stuff. Her husband had left her with two young daughters, Marsha and Blair, after 8 years of marriage. Instead of being the stay-at-home Mom she had imagined, Tara got her Teaching Certificate and become a high school history teacher. Her ex, Gene, a successful doctor, paid child support and deeded the house to her, so with her teacher's salary, she and the girls were financially comfortable.

Then Tara met Ken. He was charming, sweet and got along beautifully with the girls. As the years rolled by Ken spoke constantly of the future, a future that included him and Tara growing old together. They talked about marriage, but job transfers keep Ken moving around the state. He had a well paying job that promised a good retirement plan. Tara did not want to uproot the girls while they were in school and so they put off getting married until the kids finished school. For ten years Tara lived with an imagined future that promised happiness and financial security. She continued to teach and contributed to the standard pension plan, but was only marginally interested in the investments. Then the dream was shattered

"Uh, Tara," began Ken on their nightly phone call. "I've decided not to come to see you this weekend. I have some, ah, business I need to take care of here."

"But, Ken we have plans to take the girls to the new theater on Saturday," responded a puzzled Tara.

"Why do you have to put so much pressure on me, Tara? You can take the girls yourself," Ken snapped.

"Ken what's the matter? You always come on the weekend. Oh course I'm disappointed, but you have no reason to snap at me like that," Tara says.

"Tara, I don't like the way things are going."

"What does that mean, Ken?"

"I guess it means, I'm tired of all your demands on me. Maybe we need to take a break,"

"A break! What do you mean? Where is this coming from?" cries Tara.

"Just what I said, Tara. I've got to go now," says Ken hanging up the phone.

In one unexpected telephone conversation, the entire texture of Tara's future had changed. Six weeks later Tara got a call from a friend asking if she knew Ken was getting married next month.

Suddenly Tara was on her own. The retirement she had envisioned with Ken was no more. The retirement money she had planned on was also gone. Now Tara had to regroup and begin making her own plans for financial security.

Myth: A Man is a woman's "financial plan."

Why do women so often see the MAN in her life as her "retirement plan?" Even after divorcing, Tara still did not take full control of her and her daughter's financial security. The deeply held myth that a MAN is the answer to a woman's financial security is one of the primary causes of financial dependency in women.

As was proven in Tara's life, there is no man that can be a guarantee of a woman's financial security. In fact there are no guarantees of any kind in life, so taking responsibility for yourself is necessary.

Chapter 11

The "Stay-At-Home Mom"

At some point in most women's lives we find ourselves alone at home with only our children and/or housework to identify us, and we think no one else understands us. Well, ladies, we all understand.

Part of what is happening is that we lose any sense of "real" identity. Our self seems to merge with our children and husbands. The natural result is a feeling of dependency. Dependency is a pathway to financial disaster

Brenda, at 21 years of age, found herself the full time stepmother of three little girls, ages 2, 4 and 6. The "man of her dreams" claimed undying, forever love and asked her to marry him. Shortly after the wedding, he became the custodial parent for his girls. Naturally, Brenda, being the loving wife, was the one who really became the full time parent. She gave up her job to be the caregiver, while her new husband continued building his career and, by the way, his retirement plan.

For 12 years Brenda was the "stay-at-home" Mom of the girls and a baby boy born a few years later. It was her "job" to be home and her husband's job to be the breadwinner. During this period her name was 'Joanne, Becky, Lois and Shawn's Mom'. Or the other, ever popular, 'Sammy's wife'. She had no personal income, built no retirement fund and was developing no business credentials. Sammy was providing financially for the family, but also continued to develop his career and financial future.

At year 13, Sammy ran off with the former best friend leaving Brenda literally high and dry. Now 34 she had to battle for some financial assets in the divorce without having any income or savings with which to pay for a good attorney. In addition she had to find a job to support herself and her son. A 13-year gap in your resume makes that really difficult.

Living in a one-bedroom apartment with a little boy, finding and paying for childcare and restarting her life on an entry level salary was no fun. Reestablishing her own personal identity and self-confidence as a businessperson was a huge challenge.

Why do so many women find themselves in similar situations? Some of the money myths feed into this scenario. The messages we hear playing in our subconscious minds include;

Myth: "A women's place is in the home."

The implication here is that we cannot be multi-taskers. Rubbish! That is one of the things that enable us to be Moms and wives, in the first place. Also, this implies that we are not capable of understanding anything beyond "the home." Wrong! Delete This Message!

Myth: "A husband takes care of his families financial needs."

How unfair is this to the male gender! It is also unfair to us. I remember one dreadful night; my husband of many years came home from work literally in tears and told me that he could no longer live with the pressure of working in a high power job for a company that was expecting him to do things that he found unethical, even for the big salary they paid him. Our discussion revealed how this message, which played in his head from childhood, was literally killing him physically and emotionally. Because the same message had played in my head, I had never really questioned that he HAD to do what he did because it was his responsibility. What a shock I was now facing without being prepared. Hit Delete!

Myth: "A man must make more money that his wife"

Say out loud, "EGO is not the <u>only</u> important thing in life." Marriage and taking care of the family is a team effort and if either or both refuses to operate that way because of this message, you and your family will eventually suffer. Play your part. Be a responsible teammate.

Myth: "The husband is the one that needs a good credit score and takes care of the business issues for the family"

What if he leaves or dies? Now what? If he has a problem with this ask him how he would feel if credit scores were only in your name. This should take care of that.

Myth: "Woman are not supposed to worry their "pretty little heads" with business concerns"

AGHHHH! This is the 21st century. Get over it and Delete.

So, how can a stay-at-home Mom whose primary responsibility is caring for the family and home avoid this pathway to dependency?

Think differently!

Chapter 12

The Empty Nest Woman

When I was a junior in high school, my Mom, who had not held a job outside of our home since I was born, decided it was time for her to go to work. At 37 years old, she enrolled in adult education typing and short hand classes so she would have marketable skills. She took the Civil Service Exam and applied for a clerical job at NASA. The man who interviewed her was not inclined to hire her, but she made a rather desperate appeal to "just give her a chance." He did. This was in 1966.

Her reason for going to work had little or nothing to do with money and everything to do with "getting a life." My Dad didn't seem particularly thrilled about Mom's decision, but I suspect she offered him no choice in the matter.

As the years passed Mom became more clearly her own person. She stepped out of the shadow life of mother/wife and into a persona that was sharply defined as an individual with her own needs, desires and dreams.

When she reentered the job force she expected to be paid fairly (by 1966 standards) for what she did, but beyond that, money was not an issue even though Dad made a very moderate income by any standards. The things that drove her were based in feelings: she wanted to feel good about herself. She hoped others would feel she was valuable and she needed to feel more broadly productive than being "just" a housewife and mother offered her.

Being wealthy was not and is still not very high on Mom's priority list. She frequently gives or "loans" what extra money she has to others, because it feels good to her to do so. This is a women who in her 30's could not have been driven by riches and now in her late 70's still sees no reason to be overly concerned about wealth.

Where riches are concerned, Mom, a devout Christian woman, truly believes the tenants of the Bible, such as:

- It is better to give than to receive
- God will provide
- The love of money is the root of all evil

These "religious" based myths control many women's perspective on money.

The basis of a woman's value system can conspire to prevent her from acquiring wealth by making her feel that money is inherently bad. Do women have to reject wealth, because it's bad for them?

Let's examine the premises.

Myth: "It is better to give than to receive."

That is surely true if you are the "receiver." But, does it imply that it is NOT good to "get" for oneself? Common sense dictates that in order to be able to GIVE you must first have something to give. If your value system includes contributing to the wellbeing of others, then why not strive to earn more so there are more resources to share? Instead of using this myth to avoid becoming financially successful, realign the premise to empower you to actively gain wealth so that you can fulfill your imperative to give to others.

Myth: "God will provide."

Yes, BUT……….. Whatever your religious leanings, it's hard to find real evidence that a supreme being put us on this earth to sit back and be tended to hand and foot. Again, this concept should never excuse us from striving for success financially, but instead remind us that we were created with minds, bodies and spirits that are creative, inventive and motivated to improve ourselves and the world. God has provided all of the "raw materials" we have an obligation to use those materials optimally.

Myth: "The love of money is the root of all evil."

What's to Love? Money is not an end unto itself, but a tool to do what has to be done. Making money does not equate to loving it. Those folks, who use money as a false measurement of their human value, are in a world of their own. We do not have to go there, but neither should we go to the other extreme of using this scripture to bless unnecessary poverty or even excuse lack of financial motivation.

Thank goodness my Dad lived long enough for Mom to earn her government retirement benefits. Had he not Mom would have needed a lot more than being able to "feel" better about herself. Money to survive would have become an issue. Thinking the "right" way about these myths offers freedom to say, "I want to and should make money," and the power to aggressively pursue wealth.

Chapter 13

But, I'm an Intelligent Woman

After 30 plus years of marriage, Annie, a highly educated and successful women, found herself ready to step out of a marriage where love seemed to have evaporated. She was confident in her ability to make a comfortable living and felt she had a good understanding of her finances. There was only one problem: when it came to splitting the marital assets, her husband wanted to keep the house. To be "fair" he suggested getting an appraisal and paying her half of the estimated appreciation. This was all well and good, except that six months after the appraisal and payout to her, he sold the house for an extra $100,000. When Annie confronted the ex about the discrepancy his response was, "you accepted the appraisal and the payout. That's all you get."

Annie finds herself angry and frustrated. Her comment to me as she related this story was, 'how could this happen? I'm an intelligent woman."

The fact is *she is very intelligent*, but she did not understand the realities of real estate values and appraisals. But her ex did. Annie was well informed in her areas of expertise, but not about enough general financial matters. To add to that Annie continued to believe that after 30 odd years of loving someone, she knew him and could trust him with respect to money.

I have another friend who's ex misrepresented the value of other types of investments. She also was short-changed in the divorce settlement. Why does this type of situation arise so often? There are a couple of myths that feed this scenario.

Myth: "He is the father of my children, of course he will not cheat me out of what is legally and morally mine, even if I did not bring as much income into the household as he did."

When it comes to money, men tend to feel that they DESERVE more, because they were the primary breadwinners. Add to that the fact that the Ex believes and states that SHE will find some other man to take care of her. Heap on the very top the fact that you are now HISTORY for him.

First, whether a woman was a full contributing financial partner or not, she certainly contributed whatever value she and her husband deemed appropriate. That could have been as primary caregiver to their children, or working part time to allow her the freedom to be their volunteer representative in the community or religious organization. It may have been that she was the one willing to give up her job or business to move every time he had a better job offer, or be available to support him as the "corporate wife."

No matter what the situation she deserves and has EARNED a right to a fair apportionment of the marital assets. Then, of course, there is the issue of women's pay over the years being less than that of men. This certainly does not mean she can be short changed in the divorce settlement, too.

Secondly, what does HER future after HIM have to do with anything? It does not.

Thirdly, once you split most men tend to move on quickly. That often translates into you no longer being his responsibility in every meaning of the word.

Myth: "An intelligent woman does not need to know about everything."

Clearly, no one can know everything. But as women, we must be familiar enough with all financial matters to know the basics and be able to ask the right questions to protect our own financial interests. For example, in Annie's case, she would have benefited by understanding the realities of appraised values of real estate and how ups and downs in the market should be affecting values. It is important for woman to understand Real Estate, Stocks and Bonds, Retirement Plans, and tax issues among others.

Myth: "Men are *worth* more than women"

Lawyers, judges, friends and family members who were raised with this underlying belief make it difficult for women to get fair financial treatment. We cannot let these bias' impact our financial destinies. We have to speak up and demand to be "valued" equally.

No matter how smart or worldly we think we are, the hidden messages still color our vital decision making processes. Awareness is our first line of defense.

Chapter 14

But, I Put You Through Law School

"You can't be serious," growled Jonathan. "I worked hard to get were I am today and I will not agree to give you half of everything. All you've been is a housewife for 20 years."

"A housewife!" blurted Katherine in disgust. "Who put you through Law School? Who gave up her career to raise OUR kids? Who entertained all of those clients and kept your laundry and home in order? I AM WORTH as much of what WE have as you are."

"How did it come to this," Katherine asks herself." I did everything a wife and mother is expected to do and more, but now I'm not WORTH half of all that we have built together. What went wrong?"

Just out of college and in love Katharine and Jonathan were ready to get married and begin the wonderful life they had dreamed of and talked about for the last three years. They both found good jobs, Katharine in the insurance industry and Jonathan in county government.

After a couple of years Jonathan began to see that his career path was limited and decided that a Law Degree would be the answer to his future success. Katherine, seeing the financial value of a Law Degree, agreed with Jonathan that the three-year sacrifice both economically and in delaying the start of their family, would be a great investment. Besides she had a good job, with nice benefits, that would provide for them if they just tightened their belts. The decision was made.

The three years went by quickly with Jonathan busy studying and Katherine working all the hours she could get to pay the bills and tuition. At the end Jonathan was offered a prime position in a great firm. His career was on the way. Because of the solid starting salary he was offered, Katherine could now focus on starting the family they both wanted.

Over a 25-year period Katherine gave birth to three children. She and Jonathan took pride in watching them grow and develop into well-rounded individuals with bright futures. Through all of the soccer, baseball and ballet years, Katherine made certain that they were cared for and nurtured.

As Jonathan law practice grew, Katherine was always ready to host dinner guests, plan Holiday gatherings, chair local charity and PTA events. She made sure that Jonathan had a comfortable home and soft shoulder to lean on when needed.

Although Katherine ran the household, Jonathan insisted on have the firm's accountants handle their personal bills. As the practice grew and income grew, Jonathan had a former college buddy handle his investments and retirement planning.

As their youngest child headed off to college, Katherine began to find too many empty hours. It seemed that Jonathan was always busy with work or golf and an ever-increasing numbers of out of town business trips.

Then just before Thanksgiving Jonathan dropped the bombshell.

"Kate," he began, "I don't want to be married any longer. We've grown apart and I need to find a new life. Besides, now that the kids are grown, you need to find something to do with yourself. You need to get a job."

Stunned Katherine stammered, "What do you mean? How can you just decide to destroy all that we've built without even talking to me about it? How dare you!"
"You're tough, Kate. You'll be fine," Jonathan declares coolly.

"How can I be fine, you jerk?" Katherine cries. "All I've done for 25 years is take care of everything so YOU could do whatever you wanted to. You said I needed to be home with the kids and take care of our home. I haven't worked an outside job in all these years. What do you expect me to do now?"

"Don't worry. I'll give you enough money to tide you over until you can find a job."

"You'll GIVE me money,' Katherine says sarcastically. 'It's my money too."

"Not really," Jonathan answers smoothly. 'I'm the one who worked for all of it, not you."

"We'll see about that," Katherine retorts.

This story plays itself out in a variety of versions over and over again in our society. College educated, intelligent women find themselves in this type of situation and ask, "How could I have let this happen to me?"

The messages that Katherine accepted as valid all those years were not BAD messages. It is when women like Katherine accept these financially disempowering messages as the ONLY right messages that financial disaster often results.

Since statistics prove that there is no guarantee of a lifelong marriage, then as women we must revise the scripts we follow, while still preserving the values of family and home. Let's look at Katherine's situation.

Myth: "A woman should selflessly sacrifice for her family."

This sounds very altruistic, but in fact it is more like martyrdom. Instead of a woman "giving up" everything for her man and family, the issue needs to be reframed into, "what will both partners be willing to sacrifice, in order to achieve our collective goals of family, fulfilling careers and financial security?" Then the dialogue from day one is revised to encourage both man and woman to assume their agreed upon roles for the mutual benefit LONG-TERM of both.

Myth: "A woman can relinquish responsibility for financial planning to her husband."

In a loving, trusting relationship, women have been conditioned to believe this is reasonable. Especially when a woman is baring the primary responsibility of home and family, this even seems fair. The rub, however, is that if you do not actively participate in financial planning, how can you know what the family asset picture really looks like? Further, what you don't know CAN hurt you.

When a life-changing crisis such as divorce or the death of a spouse occurs, that is the worst possible time to find out about the family financial picture. Women need to grasp the importance of being a full partner when it comes to financial planning and investing, budgeting and savings, and retirement planning. Being lulled into complacency about financial matters by a spouse who "knows about such things" is irresponsible. As is relinquishing your right to know all of the details about family finances. Every responsible adult has a moral obligation to look out for his or her family's well being. Financial well-being is paramount. Therefore women need to assume responsibility for understanding financial issues and insist that it is their obligation as well as their husbands, to keep up with all of the financial details in the family.

Myth: "A good wife should give up working to raise her children."

Never in the history of humankind have mothers not WORKED. From the time of hunting and gathering societies, up to the present, women have always done both; raised the children and worked. Just because the work does not always involve going off to an office everyday, does not change that.

For example, at the turn of the century, a woman living in a more agricultural society, both raised the children and labored from sunup to sunset, just like her husband working the farm, feeding the animals and people, and keeping house. A man and woman's efforts were both necessary in order for the family to survive and thrive. In the 1950's typically the husband went out to work and the wife still took care of child rearing, while manually doing all of the labor necessary to keep clothes made, mended and cleaned. She managed all of the shopping and cooking as well as house keeping activities. Again, both partners were crucial to the welfare of the family.

Today, we find ourselves in a high tech society, where housework and laundry take a fraction of the time. Our children still need attention and care, but modern conveniences make even these activities less time consuming. Additionally, once children reach early school age, many hours are available for other activates.

So, can a woman be the attentive mother she and her husband wish her to be, but still create productive income? Never has it been easier to answer YES to this question. Both men and women have enormous opportunities to design careers and family care to meet the needs of the children and their parents. In the later chapters we will explore some alternatives.

Chapter 15

The Self-Employed Woman

Jim and Mary are casual friends who decide to create a new business venture. They brainstorm together, talk about the plans for their enterprise and explore all aspects of the venture together. Then the time comes to create a corporation. Jim tells the attorney that he wants controlling interest, because.....well he thinks he should have it.

When Mary finds out she feels that it is unfair. She has to decide how to address this with Jim so that he will not get angry and walk away from the business opportunity. So she decides that rather than demand her fair share, she will suggest that they form two companies and divide the business responsibilities and activities into those two entities. That way each of them will have "control" of their own parts of the endeavor.

Mary tells Jim that she feels that she has the right to have control of her own portion of the business, and rather than wrestle over shares of one company recommends the two-company solution. Jim's response is, "that's a great idea. It seems fair and reasonable."

The difference between what just transpired is that Mary told the truth while trying to preserve the relationship, but Jim took a different tack. He, not willing to deal with any conflict or confrontation, is simply dishonest. The result is that Mary assumes that what Jim SAID was what he meant and proceeds to devote time and energy to the endeavor.

However, what Jim really thought about Mary's idea was, "I will not have the control I need and cannot trust Mary to not betray me." Consequently, Jim proceeds to redesign the business plan excluding Mary while maintaining a façade of business as usual. At the point where the first customer enters Jim takes over and informs Mary in short, curt terms that he already has the "other parts" she expected to handle cared for himself.

Had Jim said to Mary at the beginning that he was not agreeable to two separate companies, they would have negotiated an HONEST agreement or both decided to part ways. Instead, Jim was the one who reinvented the business using, by the way, all of Mary's input and moved forward dishonestly to cut her out of the opportunity. Mary, because of her truthfulness and belief that Jim was trustworthy, is blindsided and cut out.

What messages could Mary have in her subconscious that precipitated this scenario?

Myth: "I am a woman and responsible to create conciliation not conflict."

By heeding this myth's message, Mary only delayed conflict. Not only that, but the outcome was likely a weaker business for both parties. If instead, Mary had acted on her rational instincts and dealt with Jim's demand for control openly and directly, they may not have come to an agreement, but they would have both then been able to proceed with their businesses with clear understanding. In the end they would have both benefited.

Myth: "Men need to feel stronger and more powerful than woman."

Why? Because we woman feel inferior? Or are we afraid that someone will not "like" us? Perhaps we simply lack the self-confidence to expect fair treatment in the business world. The only way to get past these powerful messages is to build our own credibility. Feel the power of personal success. Stop looking for personal validation from others, particularly men.

Myth: "Maintaining a man's superior ego is more important than rational business arrangements."

Many men may act this way, but if we all evaluate business success in terms of potential financial rewards, we can get past ego. For example, if Mary had chosen to confront the control issues directly using hard, cold dollars instead of worrying about feelings and avoiding confrontation the outcome would have likely been an agreement between equal parties for superior success for both.

Myth: "Men treat women the same as they do other men in business situations."

Let's rerun the scenario with John instead of Mary. In the above scenario had Jim demanded controlling interest, John would have had no concern about preserving the relationship. He would have said, "Hell no, I deserve as much as you do. In fact if you want control, let's form two companies and split the business." To which Jim would have said, "No way, that won't work because I think you would eventually leave me hanging." After which John would say, "What, you don't trust me?" At this point they would either part ways or negotiate a workable agreement.

So, what is the difference between the two situations? Only the fact that Mary was honest and trusting, but Jim could not be honest with a woman. With John, another guy, there would not ever be the consideration of being anything but honest and forthright.

Do not ever assume that there is common understanding between man and women. THAT IS NOT A MYTH.

Chapter 16

The Female Executive

Women in top executive positions often find themselves conflicted. As a person in a clearly defined leadership position, they need to act in a strongly assertive manner. However, being TOO pushy or taking the limelight often subjects them to resentment from both the men and women they direct. Therefore, women in top job positions often find themselves in lose-lose situations.

After 20 years of working her way up through the ranks, Katharine finally found herself in an Executive Vice-President position. She was in charge of the Marketing division of a Fortune 100 company, with her sights set on the President's office. As is usually the case, Katharine was surrounded by all male colleagues. She had great ideas about how to move the company forward and was anxious to implement them.

As the months passed, exposure and results were improving by leaps and bounds. Because of the success of her programs, Katharine began to get a lot of attention and was becoming something of a media personality. Wall Street was rewarding the company with rising share prices, and the public awareness of products had skyrocketed.

On a particular Friday morning during a top-level staff meeting, the President suggested that Katharine should "tone-down" her public image and stay more in the background. A few weeks later, Katharine overheard a conversation between the Sales and Operations Executive VPs, both men, referring to her as "Princess Katharine."

As a result of these and other subtle hints, Katharine began to question herself. She wondered if her job was in jeopardy, but then discounted that as absurd since the results she had created were so favorable to the company. What could she possibly be doing to incite the kind of responses she was seeing and hearing from her colleagues?

The people in her department clearly liked and respected her and her abilities. She was a team leader who gave her staff direction, but not demands. She was careful to present her position and always provide back up for her ideas. Besides, she always allowed her group to have input. The numbers showed all of this was working and working well. So, why this climate of disrespect and belittlement from her peers? When in executive staff meeting, she was respectful of her coworkers ideas and opinions and did not hesitate to make a change that others convinced her were warranted.

Then on that fateful afternoon she was called into the Presidents office, where sat the Chairman of the board and several other board members. Without any fanfare she was advised that the firm no longer needed her services. When she asked for the reason, she was told that the others did not consider her a "team player." Further, Katharine was told that her colleagues did not view her as a strong decision maker and thus, the company felt the need to look for a stronger person to fill the Marketing VP slot. When Katharine tried to defend her position by highlighting the major value her division had contributed to the companies rising success, she was advised that the success was because of a company wide effort and she appeared to overvalue her own contributions.

Katharine had walked into the company as a rising star and was leaving in apparent disgrace. Despite the nebulous reasons she was offered for her firing, nothing made sense to her. How could she have been caught so unaware by these actions? How would she recover from such a disgrace, both professional and personally? What did Katharine miss? How did the scripts she carried in her head effect this situation?

Myth: "Good leadership should be inclusive, not dictatorial."

Based on the model of conciliation and consensus building women learn from childhood, Katharine was unprepared to interact with male coworkers who saw this as weakness. As Katharine worked on a decision making model that empowered others to participate in the decision-making she was viewed as having poor leadership skills, regardless of the great results.

Men in leadership positions tell others <u>what</u> to do, Women tell others <u>how</u> to do. If the vast majority of her colleagues are men, how can a woman operate in this maze?

First, examine the matter of leadership. The difference between Katharine's style of leadership and her male colleagues is neither good nor bad, right nor wrong. It is a realistic fact of corporate life however, that as long as the male model prevails as the "right " model, a woman often finds herself misunderstood and under appreciated, as Katharine was.

Given the fact that women in executive positions are a small minority, how can a woman ever win? Achieving outstanding results is rarely the answer. Being view by one's subordinates as "good," does little good. So, how, without compromising our values, can a woman succeed?

Katharine needs to adjust the perception of her style. Instead of highlighting her process, she could focus on purely results and HER decisions impacting those results. It is possible to encourage and reward her division by being conciliatory and a consensus builder, BUT when interacting with her male colleagues, it is she who made the final decisions. Might a company suffer somewhat if Katharine changes her approach? Possibly. But it certainly suffered, as did she by being dismissed.

Myth: "Respect is something earned"

Women are led to this belief because we are trained to first "do good" then you will be rewarded. Men in turn are raised to respect Dad simply because he is the man of the house. The additional message conveyed is that position alone conveys respect on men. Mother works to "prove" her love and value everyday thus displaying a wish for respect, not an expectation of respect. Men expect respect as their due, women try to EARN it.

Katharine worked hard to achieve results, attention and kudos, that she assumed would earn her respect as the Marketing VP. This implies insecurity to her male colleagues. Again this is seen as a sign of weakness.

What's the alternative here? Katharine has to learn to "take the field." Her male colleagues, who operate on a sports team mentality, respect someone who exudes confidence and panache. The classic "fake it till you make it," is a valid approach in this type of situation.

Myth: "Decisions must be supported."

A man will assume his decisions will be accepted, a woman will try to explain and convince others of her decisions. This goes back to the messages of about authority. If a person, man or woman, reaches a position of power, they are expected to "assume" authority. Women are formatted to seek permission and approval. Katharine needed to grasp the fact that by putting her in the Marketing VP position, she needed to assume the mantle of authority and display it, especially toward her male colleagues. Anything less is a sign of weakness and the strong will eventually circle her for the kill.

Myth: Flexibility is a core value."

Women equate flexibility especially in the business arena as being in tune to changing conditions and being willing to adapt. The challenge is not necessarily that this is incorrect, but it is again a matter of apparent style. A man will often stick with his decisions until the end and "save face" while a woman will constantly challenge and reevaluate her decisions in the presence of others.

Women need to find techniques that allow for reevaluation, while being perceived as a consistent and strong decision maker. Again, it can be a matter of being less transparent while evaluating decisions. Then when changing or adjusting a position, doing so in a more declarative, rather than questioning manner. For example, Katharine can monitor and adjust the details without discussion of those small changes. Then when a major shift is called for she can walk confidently into the conference room and "tell" her colleagues that she has made a decision to change directions. The terminology and attitude alone change the perception, while allowing her to be true to her values.

Chapter 17

The Widow

"Lindy, something wrong with your Dad," the phone call begins.

"Mom, what do you mean?" a panicked Lindy responds.

"Honey I don't want to scare you, but Dad sounds strange when he tries to talk and his left hand isn't working quite right."

"Are you at the hospital, Mom?"

"No, Dear. Daddy thinks we should wait awhile and see if things clear up"

"Mom put Dad on the phone," says Lindy in a barely controlled voice.

"Lindy, I'm going to be Ok," Dad slurs. "It's probably nothing."

"Dad, I love you. Put Mom back on the phone," Lindy moans.

"Mom, stay on the phone. I'm going to call 911 on my cell and get the paramedics over there now," Lindy says.

"But, Honey, I think you might be over reacting," cries her Mom.

"Just hold on!" demands Lindy.

"Mom, they are on their way. I'm going to stay on the line with you until they get there. Then I'll meet you both at the hospital."

Bob and Sharon Everest, Lindy's folks were married 48 years. They had a comfortable life, with enough money every month to pay the bills, plus a little left over for traveling in their motor home. Both had worked long and hard earning pensions and access to insurance. Now in a few short minutes life changes.

"Mom, where's Dad?' Lindy asks as she comes running into the emergency room.

"I'm not sure," says Mom blankly. "I had to drive myself after they put your Dad in the ambulance. Now no one will tell me what's going on."

"Mrs. Everest," calls a white suited woman. " The doctor needs to speak you. Come back here with me, please."

As Lindy and Sharon follow the nurse, they are overcome by an unspeakable dread. Bob has had a massive stroke and dies. Sharon wonders vaguely, how she'll ever manage without Bob. Lindy is hit with the sadness of lose and fear for her Mom.

Two weeks later after the funeral is over and other family members have returned to their lives, Sharon sits alone in the living room trying to decide where to start. There was a life insurance policy somewhere. There were the hospital and doctors bills to deal with. She remembered that there were some CDs at the bank and a small stock account at a local brokerage. And she had to contact Bob's former company to sort out his pension. Also, Lindy had reminded her that Bob's will, which was in the safety deposit box, she thought, needed to be filed. It was overwhelming. All she could think was "how could Bob have left me like this. I don't know about these things. He always handled everything."

Not sure what else to do Sharon headed to their bank. Surely the nice lady who they always talked to there would help her. Ms. Handly was always so sweet.

"Good morning, Mrs. Everest," greeted Ms. Handly brightly. " How are you today? Is Mr. Everest parking the car?"

Stricken, Sharon, whispers, "He died week before last. I really need your help."

"Oh, I 'm so sorry," cries Ms. Handly. "Please sit down and let me do whatever I can to help."

'First, I think I need to get the life insurance policy and Bob's will out of the safe deposit box. Then take care of the CDs that are maturing"

"Oh dear," exclaims Ms. Handly." I'm afraid that the box is only in Mr. Everest's name. You can't go into it until you get an OK from the Probate Court."

"But, how do I do that?" moans Sharon. "I feel so lost."

"I can help you with your CD money though," offers Ms. Handly. "Let me take you to see our investment specialist Ron Bliss. He is very nice and will take good care of you."

"Ok," answers Sharon, not knowing what else to do.

"Ron," says Ms. Handly. "This is Mrs. Everest, one of our best bank customers. Her husband recently passed away and there are CDs maturing. Please help her take care of that."

"Mrs. Everest, please accept my condolences," says Ron offering her a seat. "Let me look up your accounts and see what we need to do for you."

'Thank you, I really have no clue what I need to do. My husband always handles, I mean handled, these things," replies Sharon.

"Well, Mrs. Everest," Ron begins, "I see that you have two $50,000 CDs maturing in five days. Let *me ask, do you need this money to live on? Or do you plan to reinvest the money?"*

"I have our pensions and some social security to pay my monthly bills, so I guess I need to leave the money here for now," answers Sharon tentatively.

"In that case, let me recommend that you invest this money in our newest Mutual Fund. It is expected to earn much better returns than the CDs are right now. Here is a prospectus for you to look at," offers Ron smoothly.

"If you think that's the right thing to do I guess I'll follow your suggestion," replies, a baffled Sharon.

Ok, Mrs. Everest, let's just take care of all the paperwork so you have one less thing to worry about," reassures Ron.

This scenario is not only possible, but I have personally worked with women who have encountered precisely this. Women who do not have an even a basic understanding of investments, ownership rights or probate matters endanger their own well-being. At the worst possible time in their lives, they find themselves confused at best, taken advantage of or in some cases defrauded at worst. The rules that are imbedded in many women's minds that can lead to this situation include:

Myth: "My husband will always be here to take care of these things"

The irrationality of this belief is obvious, but the capacity that humans have for denial is huge. Women seem to be especially good at it. Stop it.

Myth: "Men are better at taking care of financial matters than women."

We know intellectually this is simply false. Get Real!

The time for wishful thinking is way passed. Assume responsibility for learning the basics of banking, investing, property ownership, and wills and estates. No matter what life throws at you, you have to be the ones who can answer, now what do I need to do to protect family and myself.

Chapter 18

The Entrepreneurial Woman

"So, tell me what your goal is for your new business?" *asked Amy as she and Sherry walked through the vibrant* *fall colors.*

"I'm so excited about launching my training business. By *the end of next year, I'll have a complete library of audio* *and video programs priced so that anyone can learn how* *to manage their own money without having an accounting* *degree. There is such a need in the marketplace for this* *type of step-by-step information. In addition, I'll be* *speaking at as many meeting and conventions as I can* *reach."*

"That's wonderful, Sherry. It sounds like you could be the *next millionaire."*

"Well, Amy, my five-year plan is to make enough money to *retire comfortably. I also intend to set up a foundation to* *help un or underemployed women," Sherry replied.*

"Why do you want to establish a charitable foundation?" asked Amy.

"Because there's such a need for women to have access to financial resources and information" Sherry replied. "It's so often the women who have the least access that need to most help. I want all women to be able to get the information and assistance they need to have a financially successful life. So many women are in positions where they have sole responsibility for not only themselves, but also their children. If the cycle of poverty and lack of financial understanding isn't broken soon, the entire economy will be affected."

"That sounds like a great idea, but does it exclude you from being rich at the same time? In fact how can you create a foundation and let people know about it unless you're wealthy?" asked Amy.

"You're right, Amy, I suppose I do have to have the money to be able to do it. I still think in term of the results rather than being rich, though," replied Sherry thoughtfully.

"But, Sherry," Amy said quizzically, "with such a powerful business plan why don't you want to get rich?

After all, that's what you are trying to help other people do. Don't you deserve to have the same results?"

"I feel strange telling my friends and family that I want to be rich. Do you know what I mean?" asked Sherry. "I grew up in a working class family. None of my relatives are rich. They live modestly. Most of my friends are doing OK, but are by no means wealthy, so I don't want to make them think I want to be better than them. Besides, I don't feel the need to be a millionaire. That sounds so pretentious."

"I don't think it's pretentious," replied Amy. "Will you be a different person when you get rich?"

"Of course not," Sherry laughed. "I will still be just like I am now, only I'll be able to take that trip to Italy whenever I want to."

"So, you imagine that I would think less of you if you were filthy rich, even though you believe you'll be the same person, right? asked Amy.

"Maybe I'm afraid of a couple of things. What if having a lot of money did make me act differently? Or, what if

knowing I had money to burn, so to speak, made you feel insecure around me? I'd hate that."

"What you're saying is that you feel insecure about your relationships with other people," responded Amy. "Why would you imagine that people who care about you would want anything but the best for you?"

"I guess I just want to be liked. Somehow, I also fear the changes that wealth might bring. What if people think I'm stuck-up or too important to be interested in them? If I were to meet Oprah, for example, I cannot imagine her being interested in me as a person. She is rich and famous. She has powerful friends. How could I ever measure up to that? Not that I expect to be the next Oprah, you understand," laughed Sherry.

"Maybe not Oprah, but why not imagine yourself rich and famous like her," said Amy. "Besides, if Oprah met you, who says she wouldn't want you as a friend. If I want you as my friend, Oprah should be so lucky," Amy joked. "Anyway, you sound like you need to read your own book!"

"Oh my goodness, Amy, I am doing exactly what I am trying to tell other women not to do. How can I still be

thinking like this? Its nuts. That just shows that even as hard as I am working on helping other women reframe their thinking about money and financial responsibility, I still need to be reminded, too," Sherry sighed.

****

Ladies, this just happened to ME yesterday. My friend Amy and I try to walk an hour a few days a week. We walk in a beautiful old cemetery that dates back to the Civil War. As we walk we often talk about our own lives, feelings and, of course, how to cure the ills of the world. Fortunately, she knows me well enough to challenge me like she did.

After working on this book for a year, I am still a victim of all of my own internal messages.

Myth: "Your friends will not like you if you are rich."

People who truly care about their friend or family member want them to be successful. Anyone who begrudges you financial success is not concerned about your best interest.

In the real world, there will be people around us who will try to hold you back out of envy, misunderstanding or even down right spite. You do not have to buy into their vision. Revise your vision of success, rightness and reality to see money as a great tool to:

- Insure security and comfort for you and yours
- Enjoy the life we have all been granted
- Help others.

Myth: "It is unseemly to appear to WANT money."

Why do we believe that it is unseemly to want money? In my case, Amy asked me where I was coming from. As I paused to ask myself that question, it occurred to me that what I really wanted was for her to LIKE me. Because I, like so many of you, was raised to believe that "no one likes a show off," I downplayed my dreams of wealth and minimized my future possibilities so she would not dislike me. What a foolish idea. Amy wants me to be wildly successful. Our relationship is not based on who has the most money, but on what kind of person we each are.

Myth: "It is better to GIVE (set up a charitable foundation) than to HAVE money"

The whole notion of giving rather than having comes not only from our religious upbringings, but also from a desire to "prove" to others that we are "good." We don't need proof.

The concept of self-worth is tricky. If we as women tend not to measure our value with riches, then how do we measure it? Perhaps we go back to the idea of being a "good person." If society suggests a "good woman" is one who demonstrates that she puts others before herself, then we want to see ourselves as Selfless, not Selfish.

Neither selflessness nor selfishness is rational. They are both extremes. Wouldn't it be much more rational to be secure AND giving? Before we can moderate our behavior, however, we need to moderate our thinking.

Have you ever heard someone tell a sick mother, "You must take care of yourself first, or you won't be able to take care of your family in the long term?" In an extreme situation such as illness, this advice makes sense and is perfectly acceptable. Why not apply this rationale to our entire lives?

Chapter 19

Exercise to Discover Your Hidden Scripts About Wealth and Money

Its time for you to evaluate your own set of rules that govern your financial attitudes. Answer the following questions using your first thought. There is no right or wrong answer. These questions and potential answers are meant to make you think about you "natural" responses. Do not look for the "appropriate" answer. Be honest with yourself. Even if the scenario is outside of your personal experience, imagine yourself in the situation and respond. Then fill in the blank following "Why" with a one-sentence response. It is the "Why's" that will give you real insight into your own internal scripts.

1. An apparently homeless man asks you for a spare dollar for food. You:

   A. Ignore him and keep walking. (2)

   B. Give him a buck without saying anything. (1)

C. Buy some food and return giving it to him instead of the money. (3)

D. You lecture him about getting a job. (4)

Why?

_____

_____

2. You are interviewing with the female HR person for a supervisory job. She asks why you left you last job. You say:

A. My goal is to use my skills to progress into management. (4)

B. I need a better paying job to take care of my children. (2)

C. My former job was a dead end position. (3)

D. Your ad said this job had flexible hours. (1)

Why?

_____

_____

3. Your boyfriend tells you he got a great job offer, but has to move 500 miles away. You:

A. Tell him how happy you are for him and begin looking for jobs in the new city. (1)

B. Ask him," but what about us?" (3)

C. You ask him if the new job fits into his long-term plans. (4)

D. You cry for a week. (2)

Why?

_____

_____

4. You are being seriously considered for a senior management position that will require travel nationally. You:

   A. Tell your husband he will need to watch the kids more so you can take the job. (4)

   B. Discuss with your husband how the new job would affect everyone's life. (3)

   C. Tell your boss that your husband would never agree, but thanks anyway. (2)

   D. Feel guilty because you really want the job, but decide you can't do that to your family. (1)

Why?

_____

_____

5. Your son's fifth grade class trip is planned for the same time as a business development seminar you plan to attend. You:

   A. Ask your husband to take a few days off to go chaperone instead of you. (4)

B. Give up your plans and chaperone the trip instead. (2)

C. Fuss and fume for a week until your husband volunteers to chaperone instead of you. (3)

D. Beg your Mom to chaperone for you so you don't have to fight with your husband. (1)

Why?

_____

_____

6. Your Mother-in-Law breaks her hip and needs care. When your husband tells you she needs help, you:

A. Call your boss and tell him there's been a family emergency and you need a week off. (1)

B. Ask your husband how he plans to deal with it. (4)

C. Discuss how you can share the work. (3)

D. Grudgingly agree to help out. (2)

Why?

_____

_____

7. A trusted friend approaches you with a dynamite idea for a new business and asks you to partner with her. You:

A. Decline because there's so much risk involved. (1)

B. You ask your husband if it's all right for you to use some of your savings to get involved in the business. (3)

C. You work on a joint business plan and then advice your family you have decided to leave your job to pursue it. (4)

D. You wish your friend luck, but silently resent that she can DO that and you can't. (2)

Why?

_____

_____

8. At a business lunch you listen to the others discuss a new stock offering that is expected to do very well. You:

A. Call your broker and ask her to research the company and let you know if you should invest. (4)

B. Tell your father about the information and ask him what he would do. (3)

C. Figure there's no sense risking your savings on a new stock. (2)

D. Didn't understand what a new stock offering was, so kept quiet. (1)

Why?

_____

_____

9. The house around the corner looks like it's been vacant for awhile. Since your neighborhood is so desirable you:

A. Walk by it every morning and wonder why it's empty. (1)

B. Go to the tax assessor's office and find out who owns it then call and ask how much they want for it. (4)

C. Tell you best friend at work about it and ask if he knows how to find out about it. (2)

D. You call your local Realtor and ask about it. (3)

Why?

_____

_____

10. The bank calls to say that your account is overdrawn. You:

A. Call your husband at work and tell him to straighten it out. (3)

B. Confirm the recent account activity online and transfer funds to cover the calculation error you find. (4)

C. Cry, because you probably spent more than you should have at Macy's. (1)

D. Hide the next bank statement from your husband. (2)

Why?

_____

_____

11. The Church is having a Building Fund Drive, but money is tight right now. You:

A. Decline to pledge any money. (3)

B. Know that everyone expects your family to contribute, so you pledge and hope to find ways to economize. (2)

C. You pledge, but never make the contribution. (1)

D. Make a minimal pledge and work to do all your family can to live up to the commitment. (4)

Why?

_____

_____

12. You have finally received your undergrad degree and been accepted into Law School when your husband announces he wants to take an early retirement and open a business that does not interest you at all. You:

A. Join your husband in running the new business and give up on Law School. (2)

B. Explain to your husband you have worked hard to get into Law School and open a law practice so he will have to run his business by himself. (4)

C. Pretend that Law School didn't really matter that much anyway. (1)

D. Ask him for a divorce because you're tired of everything having to be about him. (3)

Why?

_____

_____

13. You've just finished college and have a car payment and big credit card bills to pay. You:

A. Ask your Dad to cover your cards, since you ran them up only because you were going to college and couldn't work. (2)

B. Take a fulltime hostess job to pay your bills before you can look for a "good" job. (3)

C. Make a budget and payoff plan. Then work as a temp while looking for a job in your field. (4)

D. Move back in with your parents and take a break until the collection agencies start calling. (1)

Why?

_____

_____

14. You've been dating Alan for two years and your family thinks he's a good catch because he is an accountant. You:

A. Decide to marry him because he makes good money and is a nice enough guy. (1)

B. Plan to work on your own career a few years before marrying anyone. (3)

C. Figure you may as well get married to him and start a family instead of getting too involved in a career of your own. (2)

D. Tell your family, you can take care of yourself so you don't need a "good catch." (4)

Why?

_____

_____

15. Two of your coworkers Laura and Ralph are vying for the
    same promotion. You overhear the manager saying he is
    going to give Ralph the promotion even though Laura is better
    qualified, because Ralph has four kids to send to college.
    You:

    A. Pretend you never heard a thing. (2)

    B. Discuss it with your husband who tells you, it makes sense
        to him. (3)

    C. Tell Laura and the Human Resources Manager. (4)

    D. Wish your husband were in line for that promotion. (1)

    Why?

    _____

    _____

16. You are in unhappy marriage and decide to get a divorce.
    You:

    A. Agree to whatever conditions your husband wants just to
        be done with it. (1)

    B. Contact an attorney and get advice about how to equitably
        split your joint assets. (4)

C. Find out from all of your girlfriends how to take him for all he's worth. (2)

D. Secretly move money from your joint accounts into your best friends account to be sure you get what you deserve. (3)

Why?

_____

_____

17. Your husband of 35 years just died of a sudden heart attack. You:

A. Have your accountant and attorney work with you to transfer assets into your name. (4)

B. Ask your son what you should do now. (2)

C. Go see the nice man at the bank and ask what you should do with the insurance money. (3)

D. Panic because you have no idea how you're going to get by. (1)

Why?

_____

_____

18. Just after your second child is born, an insurance salesman tells you that your husband needs to get a larger policy. You:

A. Agree that your husband needs the larger policy. (3)

B. Ask how you BOTH should be covered to protect your family. (4)

C. Tell your husband about the call and leave it to him. (1)

D. Can't imagine where the money would come from for the premium. (2)

Why?

_____

_____

19. You are a highly skilled single businesswoman in an executive position who is being challenged by a new male board member to not act so much like a "ball-buster." You:

A. Tone it down to avoid making waves. (1)

B. Go to the man privately and ask what, in particular, he is talking about. (3)

C. Tell the other board members; it's not fair since if one of the men were being tough, it would be acceptable. (4)

D. Secretly look for a way to discredit the complainer with his peers. (2)

Why?

_____

_____

20. Money is so tight that bills are late. Even though you know your family expects you stay home with the kids, you:

A. Tell your husband if he can't find a way to make more money, you're going to work. (2)
B. Go talk to Pastor Aaron about what you should do. (1)
C. Ask your sister to watch the kids so you can take a part time job. (3)
D. Begin looking for a full time in-home caregiver and a job in your pre-children industry that pays well. (4)

Why?

_____

_____

Evaluation of results:

Add the numbers beside each of your responses. If your results are between 20 and 35, it is likely that you have very strong scripts that are holding you back. If you are between 65 and 80 your scripts may be pushing you to the other extreme. Most people will likely find themselves somewhere in the middle. That is good in general.

No matter where on the scale you land, the real meat is in your answers to the "why" questions.

Reread all of your "whys." Look for key phrases or concepts that are repeated. For example, use of the phrase "I should," "I'm expected to," "others would." "I have to" will begin to show you whether your personal expectations are based on what YOU want, feel, deserve, need; or based upon the expectations of OTHERS.

Examine your responses as though someone else had written them. What does this other person think for herself? Does she show self-respect, self-confidence; or does she sound dependent and unsure. What are the primary messages that are surfacing from her answers? List those messages.

Next, ask yourself if the messages listed and used in the responses made rational sense in the situations described. Did the messages either direct her to or contribute to a response that would have positive or negative impact on the woman's financial future? If there were children in the situation, would they have benefited or not from her choices in the short term? How about in the long run?

Are there areas of financial matters where you see a lack of knowledge, understanding or confidence? How would you and your family benefit if you were better educated in these areas? How much brighter would your future be if you understood more about finances and business? Is there any reason you cannot learn? Who is more responsible for your future than YOU ARE? How can you become the fully independent, financially knowledgeable person you need to be?

Chapter 20

What Now?

Hopefully you recognized yourself, a friend or family member in some of these stories about women in the real world today. Perhaps pieces of several stories are too familiar to you. No matter where you find yourself today you can change the future for the better. If you are a young woman just moving into adulthood, it's time to define and refine your thinking regarding your financial future. If you are a young woman tied down by the responsibilities of childrearing and home, you can start to revise your thought processes to include a better understanding of financial matters and planning for a richer future for you and your family. If midlife is where you find yourself, there are ways to reframe your approach to financial well-being and monetary success. If your later years are upon you, it is not too late to restructure your financial situation to allow for more safety and security for you and your heirs.

Before we look at how we can begin to rewrite our mental and emotional messages, each of you needs to evaluate where you are right now. Realizing how we think is not easy or clear cut. The previous assessment is a check-up of sorts. There is nothing scientific about it. The only objective of this exercise is to get you really thinking about your own response to everyday situations that relate to your own internal scripts where financial knowledge and responsibility are concerned.

I have assigned the numbers 1 through 4 to each answer. These have nothing to do with "right" or "wrong" responses. By adding up the value of your responses, you will get a sense of where on the scale your own internal messages lead you.

Next by examining your "why?" answers you can get a clearer view of what messages or rules are governing your decisions and actions. Now apply logic and rational thinking to your rules. Do they make sense? Can you rewrite the rule so that it does make good sense? If you can't rewrite it, maybe it's just plain wrong. If that's the case, remove it from your thought processes.

Chapter 21

The Bare Minimums

It's time to act. You've examined the many myths that rob you of your personal Power. You have done your personal assessment. Now let's look at the bare minimums necessary to take you from financial dependency toward independence.

Caring for your home and family REQUIRES that you think about and act on the need for financial accountability. Take charge of the family financial books. Prepare a household budget. Track income and expenses. Pay the bills. Find out about basic investments. Read books. Find out about property ownership and Estate Planning. Talk to professionals. These things are part of the process of caring for your family.

Establish your own separate credit, even if it's opening a department store credit card with a small credit limit, in just your name. Use it regularly and pay the balance every month before the due date. Open a savings/money market account in JUST your name. Make sure you are on the deed for all real estate and titleable personal property like cars and boats, which both you and your husband own.

Set up college fund for your children. Look into the 529 plan in your state for college savings. Read the small print. Ask questions until you understand all of the ins and outs.

The number one, fastest growing segment of the economy is home-based businesses most of which are Internet based. Learn how to use the Internet. If your family cannot afford a personal computer right now, take the kids to Story Time at the local public library. While they are entertained go to the computer room and go online to learn all you can about the Internet. Take a look at the massive numbers of businesses online. Many of these businesses are making huge amounts of money while the owner is working from home. There is room for you, too!

Chapter 22

It's Up To You...It's Now or Never

Life goes by faster with each passing year. At some point in the flashing years we all stop to wonder what it's about. We ask ourselves if we're on the right track, we question ourselves about our choices, we reassess and realign as needed. Reassessing our financial positions is a critical part of this process.

I've long believed that we are responsible for ourselves no matter what has happened to us along the way. Your life right now is exactly as you've chosen it to be. That can be a sobering realization. And I wouldn't suggest you argue with it. In this existence you can literally have any life you want, but you can only live it once.

That should be a wake up call.

Where are you going to be ten years from now? Twenty? You will end up wherever you decide to go. It's your choice and nobody can make it for you, and nobody will care about your excuses if you miss your dream mark.

Take this seriously. Life offers nothing except the opportunity to choose how you will live it.

Somewhere in all of our minds we hear a clock ticking. Will you wake up now and take your shot at financial success, wealth and riches? Will you make a renewed effort and work harder? Will you plan better and make better choices? I don't know, but you better know.

I can't make you learn more, make better financial decisions or impact more lives. I can't make you do anything. Nobody can. Only you can make yourself a success or a failure.

You've got one shot. Aim well, and don't miss.

It's O.K. to Want More

It's easy to see wealthy and successful people as greedy. We don't like the idea of being viewed this way. But I have a different take on greed, and I want you to hear it.

I want to replace the word "greed" with the word "more." Greed has so many negatives associated with it. It still sounds mean to me, selfish and consuming. That whole mindset doesn't appeal to me.

But "more" does.

More just means "more." Let me give you some examples: More money, more time, more life, more fun, more living, more adventure, more deals, more happiness, more giving, more enjoyment, more simplicity, more activity, more happiness, more faith, more belief, more helpfulness, more understanding, etc. Whereas greed opens one up to a slew of criticism and condemnation, who could have a problem with more?

More helps me sleep better at night. I want to make sure I give and take more from this life every single day. Blind and wild greed only takes one further into loneliness and isolation. Soon all you're surrounded with are the symbols of your excess. And happiness and peace evades you. It's been proven through countless lives spanning the eons of human history.

More brings something quite different. More is giving as well as taking. More is filling up your life and spending it rather than collecting and selfishly hoarding it.

Always seek more. More financial success. More opportunities to tell those around you that you love them. More chances to experience fulfillment in how you spend your days, more nights to watch the stars and dream of newer and more thrilling conquests.

I hope you get the idea. Read more. Love more. Live more. Get more.

What Do You Want?

To attain success you've got to have a good financial plan and stick with it. To retain success you have to know yourself. Specifically you have to know your strengths and weaknesses.

How do you find them? Don't make this rocket science. Just start making a list of what you consider to be your strengths and weaknesses. Take note of how you respond and act in the pressure of certain situations, and be deadly honest with yourself. Consider that big important events and interactions you go through on a regular basis and grade your performance.

Think specifically about how you can use your strengths to shore up your weaknesses. This sort of "self-analysis" is not difficult to do but is something that few of us actually make the time for. It can yield real helpful insights.

Write this stuff down. Written words have some sort of magic on our inner lives that we need to harness for ourselves. When it's written it's real.

And by all means consider the input of others. It's not odd, and in fact probably really smart to ask your inner circle of family, advisors or mastermind group to list your strengths and weaknesses from their perspective. Listen and remain silent. If they detect you have thin skin about the truth they'll start to shade and lie and hide the truth from you.

That's no help. When it comes to you and the truth that will set you free, be a dealer in the bloody honest truth. You may find, as I have, that's its rare and hard to find. When you find someone whose willing to share from the heart with total clarity and purpose, you've found someone very special.

By the way, reward them for their honesty. The hurtful truth of a friend is worth a thousand times the platitudes of someone who doesn't care about you.

Choices! Make Them!

Contrary to popular thought, life is actually quite fair. It always gives you the option to do whatever you like. For example, you can keep doing your same old job for the rest of your life, or stop today and go find something you love to do. You can stop being overweight, stop smoking, driving recklessly, etc. Or not. Life gives you the choice all the time.

Choices are actually not the problem. The problem is that not very many people are aware that they face these decisions and make them everyday. *They make them.* The problem is that you're not conscious of the choice. But you still decide at some level in your mind to act. Having a bunch of rules or messages in your head is not what stops you. You must choose to revise the rules so that you make rational, productive and responsible decisions. Ultimately, changing your life is all your call.

Life is very fair.

Feeling like you're being hustled along without your consent is a recipe for great unhappiness. Yet that is precisely how many people choose to live. Stop doing that.

If life gives you a choice to do something different, something that might add freshness or spring to your day, do it, if for nothing other than the practice. Your life was meant to be lived, not just twitched at from time to time. Live it! Live it big! Start making choices and take your life back!

Change

When you want something you've never had you need to do something you've never done. It always surprises me how many of us find ourselves stuck in routines that aren't producing what we want. Most of us just allow the unproductive routines to run unchecked, and then complain because nothing new is happening.

Something new will only come into your life when you make room for it by acting differently, deliberately. A totally predictable life is guaranteed when you don't change a thing about it. What are you going to get if you do exactly the same thing? Exactly what you've always gotten.

What should you change? Life is funny in this regard, and makes getting new things very easy. *Just change anything.* Literally anything: the way you speak to people, the way you drive, your hair color, the sorts of people you choose to make deals with…ANYTHING! Once you change anything you shake loose the corrosion and rust that has formed around your old life. A new change breaks new things free, and you never know what you might get.

If wealth is what you want, start by changing your outdated thoughts. Remember the script that gives you direction. Start small, daydream, picture how your life would look if you had an extra $500 per month, and then change your mind from a "less" mindset to a "more" mindset.

Now of course it makes sense to try to change things that will make a significant difference in your life. I can't tell you what they may mean for you, but take note: In this world, the responsibility for adaptation is on the pursuer. If you are pursuing a new life, begin systematically changing things about yourself and notice what the world gives you back as a reward. If it's what you want and like, keep doing it. If is not to your pleasure, change more. You can change as much as you like, and in fact should.

Attitude and Work

I hate to say this but most people in the workforce are complainers. Whether it is a daily job in the workforce or a stay-at-home wife and mom, I can tell you without hesitation that if you hate your job, do both yourself and your employer a favor and find something else to do. Something you like.

But that's where the problem starts for many. They don't really know why they're unhappy, and what it will take to get them to career *nirvana*.

Unhappiness at work or home typically happens for one of three reasons. First, *you're just simply doing the wrong thing.* You are on the wrong bus. For whatever reason you got on this road and now can't escape because of complicated factors debts, retirement issues, too old to jump into the workforce, etc. Making the change from that spot is very difficult, but always possible.

The second reason people hate their jobs is that *they're doing the right thing but doing it for people they don't like.* They're on the right bus, sitting in the right seat, but the wrong folks are driving. This is in many ways a better problem than the first because people change, situations change...and you can have some impact on these factors if you are willing to learn some new people skills and take some risks.

Thirdly, *you're doing what you like with people you like, but you've got a bad attitude.* You're on the right bus, in the right seat with a driver you like, but you just aren't sure if this is right. And you let your dissatisfaction show in your work and demeanor.

Attitude is a very personal thing. You need hope, you need vision, you need courage and you need a plan. Get these in order and your attitude will take a jump. Get active where you are. Give it all you've got. Attitude always responds to activity, so get active in your job. The world looks much happier when you're looking up rather than staring down miserably

Give Yourself Permission to Be Wealthy

Somebody once told me that your basic philosophy controls where you end up in life. If your philosophy says that poverty is good, you'll end up broke. If your philosophy is that rich people are lucky then you'll probably feel very cheated if you're not rich, and go through life angry at those lucky people.

Chances are good that if you take the time to simply analyze your own life you'll discover that you've gotten exactly what your philosophy dictates for you. You will recognize the messages and rules you've been abiding by.

But for some of us, a "life philosophy" may be something we're not real good at thinking about or finding. Here's where to start: "What are your basic core values?" What are those things that you believe, have believed, and will always believe that are unchanging and firm? Only you know what they are.

But you must take the time to evaluate these periodically. Why? Because it's from those basic core values that all your thinking and action springs. If you discover that deep in you is a core value that says you're not worth it to be wealthy or productive or successful, trust me, you'll stop yourself.

Take the time to ask yourself questions like:

- "Do I give myself permission to go all out in life and be successful?"
- "Am I really OK with devoting myself to my dream even though I may have to cut out some other things in my life?"
- "Am I going to let my basic fears (we all have deep seeded messages) be the thing that stops me from getting where I want to go in life?"

Asking yourself these questions is vital. Revealing and understanding your own core values is simply a must for attaining and maintaining long term success in any endeavor.

Be Careful Who You Listen To

Now that you are changing how you view your financial responsibility and how you view wealth, be aware that those around you still have their own mental "rules." Protect your attitude and make careful choices about whom you spend your hours with. Be especially careful. You need to assess the people you're spending your valuable and critical time with and decide if they're increasing or decreasing you.

Seek the increasers. These are the people who have ideas and solutions for you, those who encourage your vision and make room for your input and ideas. These are people that are creators and enhancers, always on the lookout for ways to help make your life better. These people are diamonds to you and you must guard those relationships carefully.

Avoid the decreasers. Those are the naysayers, the critics, those that create problems where there are none, complainers, negs, whiners and malcontents. These people have only one goal: *to satisfy their own need for a depressing life.* You can't help these people much, and inevitably if they're blindly committed to being as they are you can't help them at all, period. You're best bet is to distances yourself from them and minimize the time you spend with them.

Now I realize that some of these negative influences might be your best friends. That happens. But mark these words: you allow those decreasers close to you at your own peril. This is a law of life. And the peril may not be immediately seen. Some acids are slow acting, and the erosion these negative people can create sometimes takes a while to reveal itself. And it reveals itself in you.

It's your job to make sure this doesn't happen. Keep clear of decreasers as much as you can, and when you do have to interact with them be on guard for the negativity that swirls around them like a dust-devil.

What It Takes To Make Money?

All of life is straight commission. Even if you have a job and get paid to show up and put in time, someone in your business is out selling, right? *That's how money is made.* It's true in nature and economics: There needs to be effort at a specific place to make something happen. Money has to be actively attracted and won, or nobody eats.

Nobody ever realizes this faster than those who are starting their own venture. You make a sale (or a buy) or you don't eat. It's just that simple.

No need to get frightened about this though. America is a money buffet. Money is literally hanging out the window of every house you see, and you'll begin getting yours when you hit the streets and start hunting. Don't ever think to yourself that the system is unfair or stacked against you. There is plenty of money and deals out there. Ample for you to become as wealthy as you like.

Get in the game! It's time to stick your hand in the great big money bag called America and take some. Just don't expect that it will be delivered via room service. All life is straight commission, and if you get money from a job now it's because somebody sold something. Help yourself.

Get Outside the Box

Everyone knows what "in the box" and "outside the box" means. Inside the box means doing the conventional and standard things. Outside the box means being an innovator, a creator.

You have probably never been encouraged by someone to get outside the box and innovate. I'm sure you'll agree that most people just don't encourage you to think that way. Ninety-nine percent of people will tell you to paint the picture of your life *inside* the lines.

Do you know why? People will only encourage you as far as they are able to believe. If they can't see something, they can't encourage you to get to it. Besides, other factors enter in such as their own personal jealousy or fear that you might get something they can't have. Be very careful not to let others limitations become yours.

Let me be the first to tell you to *GO!* You have permission to innovate your brains out. Be bold and courageous and try things nobody else is willing to try. Pursue thoughts and angles nobody else has thought of. Don't take the "no's" and "can't be done's" of life as the final answer. Rather, get used to being alone on the slicing edge. Try things that seem right to you no matter what others say.

Don't be afraid to take responsibility for failures if you're failing in the pursuit of something big and untried. The world belongs to those who are casting off proper, known rules and doing new, bold, innovative things. That has life and spirit in it! That's where the fun in life is! That's flying with eagles.

Chapter 23

How Can You Become Wealthy?

If you take a look around you you'll see many miraculous things in our world. You see buildings, cars, computers, networks of all sorts, communication, medical technology, pharmaceuticals....the list is nearly endless. This is the generation of miracles. Nearly anything that can be imagined can be created. It's an incredible age if you stop to think of it.

Nearly everything you see started off in someone's mind. Take the place where you're sitting right now. At one time it was just an empty dirt lot. Then someone had the idea of a building, and they built it. Other people probably looked at the same dirt, and if they thought anything at all, they didn't act. The person who created the building you're in right this second had a vision, and created it.

The same is true for every single thing around you right now. EVERYTHING! Someone saw sand dreamed of silicon microchips, someone connected two computers that could barely add numbers and dreamed of interlocking computers all over the world, someone saw DNA and dreamed of the day we could figure out the code and save lives. Someone saw something, had a dream for it, and created it.

When people begin the process of permitting themselves to think big, to dream and see, there's just no telling what can happen. What was previously impossible suddenly becomes highly probable. But it starts with one person having a vision for something that is not there, then taking some action believing that it can actually be done. No matter how big or audacious it seems at first. They see it clearly, and move in the direction despite the admonitions of perhaps other more experienced people that say it can't be done.

The world belongs to unreasonable people that see things **and are willing to follow that mysterious propellant called a vision.** Imagine your business today. See something grander and begin the process of making a new thing highly probable.

The Great Equalizer:
The Brave New World of the Internet

It's a brave new world out there, and even I can see that the days of "business as usual" are over. We are doing more and more on the Internet, and generally it's swiftly becoming a tool that reaches even illiterate people.

Millions of real estate deals are being initiated on the Internet yearly. The number is escalating beyond imagination.

It's changed the way this business is done, and it will continue to evolve over the next few years.

Can we know where it will go? Honestly, no, but it's growing and you must get in front of the wave. If you buy and sell real estate, take a course or buy a home study course and figure out how to take advantage of this tool. If you want to be an investor, discover the multiple ways you can use the internet to find far-off great deals and begin participating in some of the bigger money making opportunities lying in pockets around the country, and literally around the world.

But let's be honest: the market is still getting together and settling down even now. In ten years the Internet will not look anything like it does today, so your job is not to become an overblown computer junky now, but become literate enough and carve out a space there now so you'll be positioned for the times when even bigger things come. And they will come.

Start small. Begin by creating your own small website. This is easy to do and there are many sources you can tap for the proper expertise. Then begin searching for good deals on the multitude of websites already in your area. They're out there right now. Find them. Try making some offers and doing deals in this unusual way. It's popular, and growing.

And not only that, this arena is desperately in need of gurus. It's an opportunity that's wide open for you right now.

Believe You Are "Worth It"

I heard it said once that people will know more about you in five minutes than you've known about yourself in a lifetime. You wear your value of yourself, what you feel you are worth, right there on your forehead, and people are reading it.

How valuable are you? One of my favorite books is *The Greatest Miracle in the World*, by Og Mandino. It's a short story and if you haven't read it, go do it. I won't give the story away but I will tell you that the greatest miracle in the world will come as a surprise to you.

Your time is valuable, your contributions are unique, and in fact you are quite irreplaceable….if you choose to be. Be careful not to demean or devalue yourself, even if by accident. The world out there is looking for heroes, people to follow and emulate, people that give them hope for better things. Are you one of those people? Or are you one that represents the lowest value one can attain and still slither by through life? Only you know how you value yourself.

Appraise your value right now. See the things that you may believe are hidden from view. You really only have one choice: Become the person on the outside that you privately, on the inside believe you can be.

I would suggest that you consider your time to be worth at least triple what you think it is today. If you make $50,000 per year, see your value at $150,000. If you go to church and pray weekly, triple it. You're worth it. If you give $20 per month to church or charities, make it $60. You're worth it. If you give your kids and hour of time a day, make it two or more. You are what you give. Give it up and live a little. You are as valuable as you make yourself, and you haven't even begun to show what you've got.

Living With the New Messages

When you make financial decisions based on disempowering messages, they become your weaknesses. Almost everything you know and do in your life is learned. This includes your knowledge of your weaknesses. Your weaknesses aren't real, someone just told you they were. *But you believe they are.*

Think of your own personal weaknesses. You can probably make a list of them. Each and every one of them is actually just opinions (usually from other people) that perhaps you uncritically accepted and came to be entrenched within your beliefs as if they were true. They are not true. They're just opinions that became behaviors that you now participate in as if they actually exist.

This is good news, if you stop to think of it. You may in fact be much, much stronger than you've been allowing yourself to be. I find this often. You may be secretly waiting for someone to come along and free you from the prison of weaknesses that you've been convinced you have, but want to be free of. Trust me: you are not nearly as weak as you've been acting. Nobody is.

This is your freedom call: Stop participating in those arbitrary weaknesses that you've come to believe about yourself. Do yourself this favor because you deserve it. There's nothing wrong with being weak and disabled, but to do it because someone else inadvertently talked you into it is silly. Get free. You deserve it and owe it to yourself.

Even a Bad Business Idea, Vigorously Pursued, Can Succeed

I've seen plenty of bad business ideas succeed because someone was working very, very hard. Even a bad idea, a bad plan, a bad deal, vigorously pursued, can succeed. Though I do not condone bad deals, there is a powerful lesson here we all must learn.

We seem to have this mistaken idea that it's the quality of the business idea that makes money. I'm here to tell you that the key factor in money-making ventures is not the venture: it's the *venturer*. Is he or she committed, prepared, diligent, organized, expecting success? These are the true qualities that make a great deal work.

Certainly there are those ventures that are easy, money-making "lay-ups." Sometimes you just can't miss, and I take all those I can crowd on my plate. But what makes money in any venture is the vigorous pursuit of a goal by a person fully committed.

For those of you who may actually wonder what's the right business for you I would suggest you look around you. In good times and bad times, in buyers markets and sellers markets, in bull and bear markets, in high and low inflation.....*in any scenario, people find ways to succeed.* In your chosen business, *do people make money?* If the answer is yes, don't ever, ever say to yourself "this is a bad business" or "the timing isn't right", or "everyone goes broke doing that." It's simply a self-delusion you must challenge within yourself.

Let me make a suggestion to you that you may need to hear: I'm going to presume that you have a few more years to live. What are you going to do with that time? Are you going to sit around and naysay, criticize and excuse yourself from life because of the timing, the economy, or the ragged state of the federal budget?

Look, you're going to have to live through all these times anyway; why not take this opportunity....this *rare* opportunity to do something good for yourself. Pick a direction and pursue it vigorously, no matter how silly or bad it might look at first to be. Many opportunities change their appearance when you go on the hunt with a mind to win.

Chapter 24

One Step At A Time

It's common to look at the successful people and stand in amazement at their accomplishments. That amazement is usually followed by wondering if I too could do such a thing.

What's not often seen in those successes are the many small steps those stars took on the trek up. You too can make the climb as long as you keep your eyes on just the next step and do the simple things well.

This is both complicated and yet very, very simple. The steps are clear: Get a simple plan, follow it and think big. Now we are back to where we started in this book.

8 Steps To Wealthy Thinking

Step #1: Understand what you think or believe and why

Step #2: Recognize the results of accepting less than full responsibility for your financial well-being.

Step #3: Decide to make changes

Step #4: Gather the knowledge you need

Step #5: Make a new plan

Step #6: Gain the skills needed to implement your plan

Step #7: Act on your plan

Step #8: Accept wealth as your right

That's it: *8 Steps to Wealthy Thinking*. It's so common for everyone to drown in details that really, in the end, make very little difference. The colors of your folders don't really matter, the kind of pen you use doesn't matter, your race, clothing limits and hair style make little real difference. The key difference is to do the simple things better than anyone else, and do them with an attitude of great expectation and genuine effort.

Experts agree that a plan with timed deadlines are crucial. So make a simple plan and set firm goals for yourself. Don't make a detailed one-year plan until you've made a one-week plan. Keep your eyes fixed on the next challenge and deal with it as quickly as you possibly can. That is the recipe for excellence and achievement.

And one more thing: when you begin feeling over-whelmed by the enormity of what you're attempting, take the next step and don't look beyond it. It sounds trite and worn but it's true: take it one step at a time and you can accomplish anything.

Chapter 25

Increase Your Knowledge

Take care not to get caught in the snare of thinking you've heard it all and know it all. You don't. *You can always learn more.*

Here is a summary of the basic knowledge every adult needs. Read the list. You know something about many of these topics. About others you may well know little or nothing. That must change. Let's start by learning about:

Money

Banking, Checking Accounts,Money Market/Savings Accounts,
     Loans, CDs

Credit

Investing, Stocks, Bonds, Mutual Funds, Other

Retirement Planning (IRAs - Roth, Traditional, Self-Directed)
     401K, Profit Sharing Plans, Annuities, Other

Insurance (Life, Liability, Fire, Health, Accident, Other)

Real Estate

    Basic Concepts, Documents, Deeds, Mortgages, Valuation

Collectables

Taxes (Federal Income, State and Local, Personal Property, Sales,

    Other

Basic Business Concepts

    Contracts

Starting a Business

Managing a Business

Basic Accounting Concepts

Wills and Estate Planning

Trusts

Chapter 26

The True Secrets of the Wealthy

Time Management

I am going to share a discovery that will probably surprise you. After experiencing a lot of success and spending time with others who have done the same I've come to believe that the secret weapon of the wealthy is this: time management.

Simply put, wealthy people value their time as their greatest asset, and spend it like money: very carefully. It's planned for, protected and carefully doled out. It's valuable to them.

This is a something everyone should start doing now. If you wait to develop this mindset until you "arrive", you're never going to arrive. You must realize that no matter what you make now, it will only increase to the extent you increase the value to place on the time it takes you to do it.

Follow some of these suggestions. Create a workable schedule for yourself and stick to it. Set five or six "must accomplish today" goals and don't do anything else until those goals are reached. Get some accountability from an assistant, spouse or friend if your time seems to drip out of your day with little accomplishment. Get yourself in the habit of noticing the passage of time and sensing that those minutes and hours are very valuable.

Ultimately this entire exercise is about putting some structure to your life. It's not necessary to overdo it, for sometimes scheduling and structure can become a time wasting obsession. But there is a happy medium that will provide you with tremendous power once you find it and discipline yourself to stick with it.

Learn to Make Decisions

Often decisions are made for us. We're not familiar with the process of taking our own lives over and making our own decisions. Especially financial decisions.

Decision-making is a craft and you must practice. I've seen many great opportunities go down the tubes because somebody was unwilling or too fearful to make a tough call. A lot of great things are stopped from happening because of a general unwillingness to make a decision.

Learn to make the call. Right or wrong it is better than waffling and wavering in the middle. Nothing happens until someone is decisive and can make a decision without looking back.

What stops most people from making decisions is either the discomfort of doing something so "out there", or a fear that something will get messed up and they'll lose in such a way as to never recover.

Let me assure you that few decisions are that big. Get in the habit of making decisions and lining up more so that your life is filled with a constant forward flow of new opportunities and not the depressing habit of looking backwards and regretting.

You can actually practice this now. Make yourself make a few quick decisions today. For example, go to lunch and decide what you'll eat in five seconds. Right or wrong, doesn't matter. Make your decision quickly. When someone asks your opinion, try doing it fast. Don't worry if it's not "exactly" what you mean, but feel the groove of assessing the facts, listening to your gut and making the call.

Will you ever regret your choices? Sure. That's normal. But the key is to have so many more great ones lined up that even if you make a few bad ones they're swamped by the lineup of great ones yet to come. Make your decisions firmly and don't second-guess yourself.

Project Charisma

We've all met powerful people. Some people just sweep into a room and you can feel their presence. They seem to fill up the place. What is this, and how can you get some?

It's called charisma, and you can easily enhance it in yourself.

These charismatic folks do three things that set them apart. First, *they are very sure of what they're doing and make certain everyone knows.* You can begin to develop this sort of certainty in yourself first by making a list of the things you're very good at. The things that you're absolutely convinced your good at. It may take you some time to develop this list, but you have to know what you excel in before you can truly begin acting like you excel.

The second thing these folks do is they've mastered the skill of feeling comfortable doing uncomfortable things. It's actually a little embarrassing to "sweep into a room" and fill it with your presence. But if you make yourself begin thinking this way, then expose yourself to the discomfort of making yourself be on the spot in front of people, you can do it. Allow yourself to feel the strange feeling of projecting power to others through focusing on your total, all out convictions of what you're doing.

The last thing they do is *that they look people in the eyes and speak with conviction.* And they don't blink. They have learned from experience how to get people to respond to them. This is power, pure and simple. But it takes practice because it too can be a little uncomfortable at first. We're far more used to speaking to others in a more comfortable way, i.e. looking away, joking, not making clear, hard points, etc. That is communication, but it is not charismatic communication.

Let yourself feel the discomfort of a firmly, more intense style of communication. Speak directly into people's eyes without wavering, and feel the strength build up within you. It's fun, and in short order you'll be walking into rooms and people will want to make deals with you!

Build Resilience

One of the key attributes of a dying person is fading resistance and failing resilience. It seems that resilience is one of those biological factors that's built so deeply into our structure that it's one of the last systems to shut off. Resilience is one of the last things to go.

I believe the identical system is at work in our minds. And much like with our bodies we need to spend time thickening our skin and systematically building resilience to the slings and arrows that will be thrown our way.

How do we systematically do this? Biologically, resistance builds with limited exposure to the thing you want your body to learn to resist (think of flu shots, mumps, measles, etc.) Internal resilience builds against the test bugs, and then when the real things come a prepared defense blasts them.

Mentally it works the same way. Take on new challenges in small but progressively larger doses. As you enter new challenges, rather than thinking how scared you are or about all the things that can go wrong, use that same imagination to wonder about how you can make the deals faster, more fun and more profitable.   That "smiling in the face of disaster" attitude can make your life very fun and very interesting.

And it builds magnificent resilience. Resilience is really nothing more than having seen it all and knowing that you can get through it.   For example, when you're very young and you cut your hand, you freak out because you think you're going to die. All kids do this.   But as you age and cut your hand a few times, you don't freak out (as much) because you know it's fixable; you're not going to die.

Jump in and permit yourself to get cut a couple of times. Let your experiences evolve into powerful resilience and strength.

Stick-to-it-tiveness

There is a common perception of heroism that is probably wrong.   Heroism, as depicted in movies and myths pit these larger-than-life characters in impossible situations, then creates against-all-odds problems which they conquer and reign.   That's the basic pattern of mythical heroism.

Real life heroism could not be more different.   Real life heroism pits very ordinary (and sometime sub-ordinary) men and women in reasonably doable situations where they take action and save someone enormous trouble and sometimes their life.   That's real life heroism.

You can be a real life hero.   All you must really do is one thing: Stick to it.   Just pick something you want to do and keep at it until it's done. That's the complete formula for creating earthshaking and life changing deeds.

I know this doesn't sound too sexy. But it's a great way to get rich. And you want to know the even better news? Anyone average person can do it; the situations aren't that tough and nobody is going to die if you fail.

Real estate, for example is simply a fast and easy way for the average American to place their names of the list of the immortal few who took their lives back. The margins of profit are so large that even if you're lazy and do mediocre deals you can still make out very well. It's not a matter of being bigger, stronger, smarter, more handsome or better bred than the next person. It's just a matter of picking a direction and sticking to it until you arrive.

So forget about becoming even more educated and capable before you jump up and do ever bigger deals. It's not about that. It's about the try, and sticking to it once you begin.

Chapter 27

Managing Your Financial Future

If there is one arena that I would strongly urge you to get a mentor or a coach it's in the arena of managing your career. There are simply too many options and pitfalls to trust your own limited judgment. And besides, you'll find most seasoned vets are very willing to share time saving and maybe career saving advice.

There are many things to be managed. Cash flow, new opportunities, entity structuring, tax consequences, retirement planning and succession in your business…the list of things you'll need good advice for is long.

How do you find this help? I'm a great believer that you should decide what you want your future to look like when you're all done, then find someone who's living that life and ask for their input. I recommend that this person be someone you really like and admire, want to emulate, and is perhaps nearly finished with their own career. That would be the perfect mentor for you.

My guess is that that person is already in your life or around it someplace. All that's needed is for you to ask them for time to help you plot the course. They'll be flattered and open to helping out. Who wouldn't be?

Then of course is the professional mentor or coach. Since I mentor people myself I know how important my input is to those who have high and mighty aspirations. I want to help them so bad, and truth be known I'm dying to see these folks succeed. I would literally do anything to help them. Anything I have is theirs.

Just be certain that the person you're receiving advice from is someone you truly emulate. Would you like to end up just like them? Make this a conscious choice. You will become who you emulate.

Conclusion

Enjoy

Wisdom, good judgment, astuteness, rationality, insightfulness, and shrewdness with money are the rights of every woman. You are capable, intelligent, teachable, and flexible. These attributes are all that you need to take control of your financial well-being. You deserve abundance. You are worth all of the wealth the world has to offer you. It is right, good and responsible to aim for riches. How you employ those riches and not the number of dollars is what defines who you are. Get in order to give.

But, never forget to enjoy your fortunes. We were not intended to live a life of want and suffering. We have been given all the tools necessary to live a life of more, better and best. Regardless of how you use your future wealth, reward yourself too.

In the couple of years preceding my fiftieth birthday, life had taken an unexpected and very unpleasant turn. I was recovering from the emotional disaster of a sudden divorce, while still in the process of healing from a serious health challenge. My last child had left for college, so my nest was totally empty. Three months before my husband of twenty-four years walk out, I had started a new business venture with partners who were counting on me to keep things rolling. I was heart sick, physically weakened, lonely, and sorting out property settlements, but I always knew that the tools, skills and knowledge I needed to be financially secure on my own were in my hands.

In the midst of all of this turmoil I decided it was time for a survival reward. So, on my birthday I walked into the local Lexus dealership showroom and announced to the first salesperson who approached me that I intended to drive a shiny brand new car out of there *today*. The salesperson asked about financial issues to which I replied "just get the car ready and show me to the financial manager's office to sign the necessary paperwork."

Within one hour, I drove a sexy two tone gray Lexus out of the showroom doors. It felt good. I was in control of my destiny. I was worth every nickel it cost. I bought it just for me.

Recognizing the truth of the revised rules and messages we've explore together in this book give you the power to be the person you wish to be; to help those who you want to help; to live the style of life you desire; and to know that you are fully responsible for your own financial well being.

It's yours. Take it. Own it. Believe it. Live it. Thrive!